Life of Governor Samuel Ward

By William Gammell

PANTIANOS
CLASSICS

Published by Pantianos Classics

ISBN-13: 978-1-78987-092-3

First published in 1846

Contents

Preface

The materials for the following sketch have been obtained principally from the letters and private papers of Governor Ward, now in the possession of his descendants in the city of New York. In addition to these, the writer has examined the legislative records and the files of ancient documents in the office of the Secretary of State of Rhode Island, as well as the published memorials relating to that period of her colonial history. His aim has been to associate the life of a worthy and a leading patriot with the important era to which he belonged, and to make the narrative illustrate, as far as practicable, the spirit which prevailed in a colony whose services in the revolution have never yet been duly chronicled.

Chapter One

The generation who peopled New England during the middle of the eighteenth century were witnesses of a series of events, whose importance in shaping the subsequent character and the ultimate destiny of the colonies can scarcely be estimated too highly. It was the age, in which was brought to a close the protracted struggle between England and France for ascendency upon this continent; in which were suffered the worst evils of the ill-devised legislation of the Parliament, and the earliest aggressions of the British ministry upon the rights of the colonies; and in which were seen the first acts of resistance that terminated at length in the war of American independence. To this generation belonged Governor Samuel Ward, the subject of the present sketch; and in the colony with which he was connected he was among the foremost of the patriotic actors in the stirring scenes of the age.

He was descended from an ancient and respectable family, of which the first representative in this country was his grandfather, Thomas Ward, who came to Newport, Rhode Island, soon after the restoration of Charles the Second. In England he had been attached to the republican party, and had been somewhat conversant with the affairs of the Commonwealth. He was highly respected in the colony, to which he rendered many valuable services, both as a private citizen and as a member, at different times, of both branches of the colonial legislature. Thomas Ward died in 1689, leaving a second wife, whose maiden name was Amy Smith, and their only child, Richard Ward, who was born a few months before his father's death. Richard Ward, the father of the subject of this memoir, on attaining to manhood, was an active and exemplary citizen of Newport, engaged in commerce, and devoting much attention to the affairs of the colony, in whose service he was distinguished for his fidelity and probity of character. He was for several years Recorder, or Secretary of State, and afterwards Deputy-Governor, of Rhode Island, and was twice elected to the office of Governor, in 1741 and 1742; after which he declined a re-election, and retired to private life.

Samuel Ward, the second son of Richard, was born at Newport, on the 27th of May, 1725. His mind was early subjected to the discipline of that best kind of education, which arises from the associations of a well-regulated family circle, of cultivated manners and liberal tastes. He was also sent to a grammar school in his native town, which in its day maintained a high celebrity as one of the best schools in the country. Here, aided, as is probable, by the instructions of his elder brother, Thomas, who graduated at Harvard College in 1733, he passed through a course of study which was probably more than usually extensive and thorough for one not destined for either of the learned professions.

For a considerable period prior to the American revolution, the ancient town of Newport was among the most flourishing commercial towns on the Atlantic coast. Its capacious harbor made it the resort of much of the foreign shipping that visited the colonies. The enterprise of its inhabitants had embarked in nearly every branch of colonial trade, while the salubrity of its climate and the surpassing beauty of its ocean scenery were already attracting temporary visitors from less favored climes, and making it what it has since become, the most delightful watering place upon the continent. Amidst its external prosperity and its intimate relations with the mother country, the society of the town is said to have been distinguished for its polished manners, and the intellectual spirit with which it was pervaded.

Here the philosopher Berkeley passed two years in maturing his generous plans for civilizing the Indians and educating young men of the colonies for the ministry of the gospel. This eminent man was much in the society of the town, and for a time assisted the rector of the Episcopal parish in the performance of his parochial duties. His active and generous spirit, enriched as it was by the most liberal culture and the noblest benevolence, must have exerted a controlling influence over every circle in which he moved. While residing at Newport, Berkeley is said to have composed his "Minute Philosopher," the most finished and the most enduring of all his writings, which has for ever linked his name with the quiet' shores of the beautiful island which was then his home. He also founded a literary and social club, made up of the gentlemen of the town, which, no doubt, was instrumental in elevating its character, and promoting a unity of feeling in relation to subjects of general concern. From this association, whose object was "the promotion of knowledge and virtue," at a subsequent period sprang the Redwood Library, which, had it been earlier started, would doubtless have received from Bishop Berkeley the valuable collection of books, which, on leaving Rhode Island, in 1731, he distributed among the clergymen of the colony and presented to the colleges at Cambridge and at New Haven.

In the midst of a community whose social and literary character was expanded by influences like these, Samuel Ward passed his boyhood and youth, enjoying, in addition, the best advantages for a common education which the colony in that age could afford. He is believed to have devoted himself to the acquisition of knowledge with earnest diligence, and to have derived from the advantages which he enjoyed, what for the time was considered a remarkably good education. His father had long been extensively engaged in navigation, and was at the head of a trading house in Newport. He was also possessed of considerable estates in King's county, on the opposite shore of Narragansett Bay, which had also received a share of his personal attention. To the charge of the same interests Governor Richard Ward directed the attention of his second son; and, by the time he had reached his majority, he had become conversant with the business alike of a merchant and of a farmer. He married, in early life, Anne Ray, the daughter of a respectable farmer of Block Island, and soon after removed to Westerly, and settled on a farm, which he received from his father-in-law, as the dower of his wife. [1]

Here, in a secluded portion of the colony of Rhode Island, Mr. Ward entered upon the duties of manhood, on a quiet plantation, which by his industry and judicious expenditures he soon formed into a valuable and beautiful estate. In accordance with the hereditary custom of his family, he also kept a store in the town of Westerly, and was often engaged in commerce both at Newport and at Stonington. In all these enterprises he was blessed with a good degree of prosperity, and early became possessed of such pecuniary means as rendered him independent of personal labor, and enabled him to devote his time and energies to the interests of his native colony, whose service was soon to demand the most patriotic exertions of all her sons. Though living in retirement, he did not withhold his attention from the public events which took place around him; and, as the subsequent course of this memoir will show, he was always sagacious in apprehending the questions at issue, and among the foremost in advocating, both in private circles and in the public offices with which he was intrusted, the interests of justice, and truth, and freedom.

[1] This lady was an elder sister of "Catherine Ray of Block Island," whose name frequently appears among the correspondents of Dr. Franklin, and to whom he addressed some of the sprightliest of his familiar letters. See Sparks's *Franklin,* Vol. VII. pp. 85 et seq. The incidents referred to in the letter on the eighty-fifth page must have occurred while both Dr. Franklin and Miss Ray were on a visit at Mr. Ward's in Westerly.

Chapter Two

For a considerable period after his settlement at Westerly, Mr. Ward appears to have devoted his principal attention to the improvement of his estate, and the prosecution of the commerce in which he had embarked. He studied agriculture as a liberal art, and soon became distinguished among his neighbors for the success with which he applied its principles. He gave much attention to the improvement of the several breeds of domestic animals with which his farm was stocked, and was particularly celebrated for the specimens he raised of the Narragansett pony, a race of horses which has now become entirely extinct, but which in that day constituted a leading article of export from the colony, and was greatly admired for the ease and fleetness of its movements.

According to the traditions which are still preserved in Rhode Island, the farmers of the Narragansett country, for a long period before the revolution, were generally men of a superior intelligence and a higher breeding than were often to be found in their brethren of the other agricultural districts of New England. Many emigrants of considerable fortune, who had come to this country in the early part of the eighteenth century, had been attracted to the beautiful and fertile farms which skirt the western shores of Narragansett Bay, and had planted there a large though scattered community, distinguished for intelligent enterprise, for accomplished manners, and for elegant hospitality. The mode of life then prevalent there combined much of the quiet and simplicity of the country with many of the characteristics of a commercial town. The distinctions of master and slave were still maintained; and negroes, most of whom were in servitude, and who then constituted nearly one tenth of the population of the colony, were to be seen in great numbers on every large estate. These features suggest to us a conception of agricultural life, and of social relations, such as would, perhaps, best be realized in our own day among the plantations of some of the upper counties of Virginia.

In retiring thus to the country, Mr. Ward by no means withdrew from the intellectual activity and cultivated society, to which he had been accustomed at Newport. There were living around him some of the leading men of the colony, whose companionship, not only in his own chosen pursuit of agriculture, but in every other sphere of life, was fitted to improve, as well as gratify, an intelligent young man. These persons formed themselves into a club for social intercourse and intellectual improvement, and were accustomed to meet at each other's houses, to bring together at the festive board the results of their reading or experience, and to discuss the public events which were then beginning to assume an unwonted importance.

In this manner, interrupted only by occasional visits to Newport, and more rarely to Boston and New York, Mr. Ward passed the years of his early manhood. Living upon his own well-ordered estate, from which, with a grateful spirit, he received the bounties of Providence, surrounded by his family and in the midst of congenial neighbors and friends, he stands out in the foreground of a picture which any man might well aspire to realize. From this retirement, however, he was soon to be summoned forth to mingle in the agitating politics of the day; and, after engaging in the fiercest strifes of the politician, and reaping all his ephemeral honors, he was at length to act an heroic part in the opening drama of the revolution.

His first appearance in the public service of the colony was in 1756, when he was elected to the General Assembly, as a deputy or representative from the town of Westerly; a post which he continued to occupy with but a slight interruption till May, 1759. In that early time the legislature of Rhode Island, though not inferior to other similar bodies either in the dignity of its forms or in the variety of the powers which it exercised, yet presented but a limited theatre for public debate. Its members were always few in number, and, being elected twice every year, they brought with them to its councils the fullest sense of the popular wishes respecting nearly every public measure. Hence their sessions were short, and their acts were usually passed with but little debate. In the proceedings of the Assembly Mr. Ward appears immediately to have taken an active part; and, though probably one of the youngest of its members, he early won for himself a wide and commanding influence. The frequent recurrence of his name upon the pages of its records indicates how intimately he was connected with the most important public measures which occupied its attention.

The irregular contest between England and France, which had been waged for more than two years in their respective colonies, had now broken out into an open war, which was declared on the part of England in May of the same year; and the several colonies were preparing to engage in it with their utmost zeal. A considerable number of French residents in Rhode Island, who had been seized by the colonial officers and thrown into the jails as prisoners of war, sent a petition to the legislature, praying for their liberation and the privilege of removing to some neutral port, and claiming an exemption, in the meantime, from the laws of war. Their situation excited no small interest among the people of the colony, and involved a principle which was likely to prove important in the subsequent progress of the contest. The whole subject, when presented to the legislature, was referred to a committee of which Mr. Ward was a member, who reported a bill authorizing the government to transport the Frenchmen in question to some neutral port, but refusing them any exemption from the ordinary fortunes of war, and requiring them still to be kept in jail; a measure which was doubtless thought to be necessary on account of the facilities they would possess, if set at liberty, of giving information to the King's enemies.

Mr. Ward was also a member of the committee for levying the annual tax, and proportioning it to the several towns of the colony, a work which was at that time considered among the most difficult and embarrassing of the duties of the legislature. So diverse were the interests and the resources of the several towns, that scarcely a year passed away without occasioning a protest from some of them against the rates which had been assessed; the agricultural community now insisting that the commercial interests should bear a larger share of the public burden, and the southern towns now complaining that the growing capital of the north was regarded by the Assembly with too indulgent an eye.

Another of the services which he rendered to the colony in his capacity of legislator, was in the investigations he made as a member of the committee on the violations of the laws of trade. The instructions which had been received from the King were urgent and peremptory, that the Assembly should "pass effectual laws for prohibiting all trade and commerce with the French, and for preventing the exportation of provisions of all kinds to any of their islands or colonies." The existing colonial statutes for enforcing the navigation acts of the British Parliament were but slightly regarded; and an extensive contraband trade was carried on by merchants in all the colonies, in defiance of the authority of Parliament, and in most instances without the interference of their own legislatures. When the state of the trade was spread before them, the General Assembly, in accordance with the report of their committee, adopted such regulations as were necessary in order to comply with the instructions of the King, and in every way in their power prepared the colony to engage in the war as it became true and loyal subjects.

It was also during the year 1756, that the legislature of Rhode Island passed its first general act for the relief of insolvent debtors. It provided, that persons who should give up their property for the benefit of their creditors, and make oath to the fidelity of the surrender, should be discharged from all claims preferred against them. The law was undoubtedly called forth by a few instances of failure, which, in the distresses of the times, had occurred among the merchants of the colony, one of the first and the most conspicuous of which was that of Mr. Joseph Whipple, a merchant of Newport, who at the time of his failure held the post of Deputy-Governor. The law which was then passed has served as the basis of all the subsequent legislation upon the subject of insolvency in Rhode Island, and does not differ very materially from that which is now in force in that state, and indeed in most of the other states of the Union.

The war with France was now becoming an engrossing subject of attention with all the northern colonies of America. It had thus far been prolific of nothing but disaster and disgrace to the English arms. The colonists had engaged in it with their utmost zeal; but, such was the delay of the ministry, and such the incapacity of the generals who had been sent to conduct it, that every year had witnessed the gradual decline of the English power in America. The French, on the contrary, were every year gaining ground, and were gradually encircling the British possessions by the lengthening chain of their military posts, and, with the aid of their Indian allies, were spreading terror and dismay through the settlements.

Immediately on the formal declaration of war, in 1756, the Earl of Loudoun was sent to America with a large force, which, together with such as should be furnished by the colonies, he was directed to employ against the French. His arrival in America was greeted by the several colonies, and Mr. Ward was appointed one of a committee to prepare an address of welcome on the part of Rhode Island. One of his first acts, on assuming the command of the forces, was to levy four thousand troops from New England; and of these the proportion to be raised in Rhode Island was four hundred and fifty. The troops were raised, and were on their march for the rendezvous at Albany; but the season was too far advanced to admit of any effective operations, and they were dismissed at the beginning of November without having been employed in actual service, but were ordered to be in readiness when summoned again to the field in the ensuing spring.

It was early evident, that the reverses which the English had experienced thus far in the war were not likely to be soon retrieved by the generalship of Lord Loudoun. He appointed a convention of the Governors and Commissioners of the several colonies to be held at Boston, in January, 1757; which seems to have terminated only in still greater distrust of the military capacity of the General-in-chief. The colonies, though commonly yielding a ready compliance with the requisitions which were made upon them, yet found serious cause of complaint in the unequal levies that were successively imposed; and the troops themselves were unwilling to be mingled with the British regulars, but demanded to be placed under the command of their own officers. Questions like these served only to embarrass the plans which the commander had set on foot, while, by the distrust and apprehension which they awakened, they added a deeper shade to the general gloom which hung over the colonies.

Rhode Island had a deep interest in the speedy termination of the war, as well as in all these questions relating to the terms of its continuance. She had already lost from ninety to one hundred vessels that had been captured by the enemy, a loss; which, according to a statement of her Secretary of State, made in 1758, was three times as great as that of New York, and four times as great as that of Massachusetts. She had added immensely to her public debt; and, in addition to fifteen hundred men, who were engaged as privateers in the war, she was obliged to maintain an armed vessel for the protection of her coast, and had also furnished to the campaign of 1757 not less than a thousand men for the service of the King. This was done at a period of gloom and dismay, when the whole number of her citizens between the ages of sixteen and sixty, then the legal limits of military service, scarcely exceeded eight thousand. It was an effort scarcely equalled by that of any other colony, for she had nearly a third of her whole effective force in actual service beyond the limits of her own territory.

In the winter of 1758, the Earl of Loudoun, finding himself still surrounded with difficulties and embarrassed by the jarring interests of the colonies, summoned another convention to meet at Hartford, in the month of February. At this meeting, Governor Greene, at that time the chief magistrate of the colony, and also Mr. Ward, and Mr. John Andrews, were appointed to represent Rhode Island. The commissioners received full and explicit instructions from (lie legislature as to the course which they were expected to pursue. In these instructions they were directed, on arriving at Hartford,

"**1.** To lay an exact state of the colony before his lordship with regard to its fortifications, cannon, warlike and military stores, the number of inhabitants, state of the treasury, and funds for supplying the same.

"**2.** To beg his lordship to lay the defenceless condition of the colony before his Majesty in the most favorable light.

"**3.** To request his lordship to make the colony such an allowance for the provisions and military stores furnished by this colony for the two last years, as will correspond with his Majesty's gracious intentions signified unto us by his Secretary of State."

The commissioners were also directed to "request his lordship that the forces raised by this colony may be under the immediate command of their own officers, and no others, except the Commander-in-chief."

To these directions, which were probably open to all the commissioners who composed the convention, the General Assembly ordered the following to be added, which was to be regarded as a private instruction for the guidance of their representatives in adjusting the quota of troops, the most difficult and delicate part of their task. "And as to what aid or number of men you are empowered by virtue of your commission to furnish his lordship with, on the part of this colony, towards the ensuing campaign, you may agree to raise one fourteenth part of the number that shall be raised by the New England colonies; but, if that proportion cannot be obtained, you are then to agree to such other proportion as shall appear to you just and equitable."

These instructions aid us in comprehending the circumstances of the times, and illustrate the nature of the questions which were at issue, while they also serve to indicate the spirit of loyalty and of sacrifice for the general good, which pervaded the people of Rhode Island.

Governor Greene was prevented by sickness from attending the convention, and the performance of the duty assigned to the remaining commissioners fell almost entirely upon Mr. Ward, who, on his return from Hartford, submitted to the legislature a full report of the doings of the convention. From this report, which is entered at length in the records of the Assembly, it appears that the Rhode Island commissioners proposed that the several colonies should furnish troops for the next campaign in exact proportion to their respective population; an arrangement by which Massachusetts would have raised two thousand four hundred and thirty-two soldiers, Connecticut one thousand five hundred and eighty-two, and New Hampshire and Rhode Island each would have raised four hundred and twenty-five. This number on the part of Rhode Island was objected to by Lord Loudoun as smaller than that which had been agreed upon by the convention at Albany, as the quota of the colony; and the commissioners were obliged to waive their proposal, and yield to the levy which his lordship demanded. They were, however, assured by the Commander-in-chief that no further difficulties should arise respecting the command of the troops, for he would take those from Rhode Island under his own especial command. The report of the commissioners was fully approved by the Assembly; the men, whose levy they had guaranteed, were immediately ordered to be raised for the campaign of the following summer. This campaign, however, furnished far better illustrations of the valor and endurance of the colonial troops, than of the skill and conduct of their commander.

Chapter Three

The period at which Mr. Ward entered upon public life in his native colony was one distinguished for the violence of the local jealousies and party animosities which so frequently appear in the history especially of small communities. The people of the southern counties of Rhode Island, from the first institution of the government, had been more or less at variance with those of the northern.

The town of Newport was at that time the only port of entry in the colony, and in point of commercial importance was one of the foremost towns along the entire Atlantic coast. It was the centre of the principal wealth, and the residence, probably, of most of the leading men, of the colony: and, though the legislature was accustomed to hold its sessions in each of the several counties, yet Newport had long been the place where the offices of state were established, and was more than any other town the seat of the colonial government. Providence, standing at the head of the navigation of Narragansett Bay, was the older town, and was rising rapidly in wealth and importance, and already beginning to dispute the supremacy of the ancient capital. Amidst these relations subsisting between the two leading towns, a mutual jealousy had gradually sprung up, which had doubtless been fostered by the aspirants for office, and strengthened by the various local interests that had been incidentally involved in the issue, until it now divided the opinions and controlled the politics of the entire colony.

Among the incidental questions upon which this jealousy had fastened, the two most important were, the policy of the government in relation to supplies for the French war, to which allusion has already been made, and the famous question of paper money, which, in all the colonies of America, was a subject of endless perplexity and embarrassment, and in Rhode Island appears to have yielded its fullest harvest of social and political evils. The whole subject of the emission of paper money in the colonies, to the statesman and the political economist, would be one of the most curious and instructive connected with their history. For fifty years, this deceptive currency spread its disastrous influence over the trade and the morals of the country, and was not wholly abandoned till the benefits of political independence had changed the relations of trade between America and all other parts of the world.

The earliest emission of bills of credit, to take the place of gold and silver in Rhode Island, was made in 1710. The colony had been at great expense in furnishing supplies for the war with France, in which the mother country had been involved ever since the accession of William and Mary to the throne. Finding the resources of the treasury inadequate to the exigency, the General Assembly, following the example already set by Massachusetts twenty years before, adopted the fatal though perhaps inevitable expedient of issuing bills of credit, and thus delaying the actual payment of the debts which had been incurred. The first emission did not exceed the sum of five thousand pounds; but this mode of postponing to the future the necessities of the present, having been once invented, was found to be too convenient to be readily abandoned. Other emissions followed in rapid succession, until, ill 1749, after the lapse of nearly forty years, the bills which had been issued amounted to not less than three hundred and twelve thousand three hundred pounds, of which one hundred and thirty-five thousand pounds were still standing against the treasury, in one form or another; and these constituted the depreciated and almost valueless currency of the colony.

Every occasion of public expenditure furnished an excuse for the issue of a new *Bank*; and though merchants were everywhere suffering from the policy, and frequently petitioned against it, and most intelligent persons were satisfied of its ruinous tendency, yet so captivating to the people is always the idea of plentiful money, and so clamorous were now the multitude of those v/ho were largely in debt, that numbers of the Assembly constantly yielded to the popular will, and in some instances, it is said, actually legislated to meet their own private necessities. The currency which was thus created tended in no equivocal manner to impair the commercial contracts, and to prostrate the commercial honor, of the whole community; while it perpetually offered to the reckless and the profligate an opportunity, too tempting to be resisted, to counterfeit the bills of the colony; a crime of frequent occurrence, though punished in Rhode Island with cropping the ears and branding the forehead of the offender, together with the confiscation of his entire estate. [1]

Such is a brief outline of the subject upon which the two political parties in Rhode Island were accustomed most frequently to divide during the period of which we are now writing. The mercantile, and what was then regarded as the more aristocratic portion of the community, were usually opposed to the emissions of paper money, while those whose fortunes and avocations placed them in humbler life were arrayed in their favor. At the head of this latter party, which was also supported by some of the leading citizens of Providence, stood Stephen Hopkins, a gentleman whose name is conspicuous in the annals of the colony, and who, both as a determined opponent in the fiercest contests of local politics, and an unwavering coadjutor in the far nobler struggle of the revolution, was for many years intimately connected with the public life of Samuel Ward. Supported principally by the northern towns of the colony, Mr. Hopkins, in 1755, had succeeded Governor William Greene, as the head of the government, in opposition to the wishes and efforts of a powerful minority who were attached to the interests of the south. The success of the Hopkins party raised to a high pitch of excitement the animosity between the two districts of the colony, and, during the years in which Mr. Ward was a member of the Assembly, this animosity was frequently manifested in the action of that body.

In the political contest previous to the election of 1757, when Governor Greene was still the candidate of the mercantile and southern party, in opposition to Governor Hopkins, to whom strong objections had been raised, the latter gentleman published an address to the freemen of the colony, in which he insinuated that the legislature, in its recent sessions, had pursued a policy hostile to the success of his administration. Mr. Ward was at that time a member of the Assembly, and took occasion immediately to come forward in its vindication. In defending it from the charges of Governor Hopkins, he reviewed the Governor's administration, and stated at large the official acts which had given offence to the people, dwelling particularly upon the conduct of the executive in relation to a cargo of sugars, which had been forfeited to the colony, and also in relation to the liberation of some French prisoners of war, which had been made contrary to the acts of the legislature.

For some cause or other, which, to one at all conversant with party warfare in our own times, it is by no means easy to assign, this vindication gave great offence to Governor Hopkins, and, though at the time occupying the chair of the chief magistrate, he immediately commenced an action for slander against Mr. Ward. The action was entered in the Court of Common Pleas for the county of Providence, the county where the Governor had always resided, and which was warmly enlisted in the interest of the political party of which he was the acknowledged chief. In order to escape the prejudicial influence of party feeling, and to secure a fair trial, Mr. Ward petitioned the legislature to remove the cause to one of the other counties. On this petition being granted, Mr. Hopkins, who was now out of office, and was doubtless suffering from the mortification of recent defeat, immediately discontinued the suit, for the purpose of evading the legislative decree, and, on the rising of the Assembly, commenced another, still in the county of Providence. At length, however, after many delays and evasions on the part of Mr. Hopkins, which could have been suggested only by feelings of political rivalry or the exasperation of disappointment, it was agreed by the two parties, that Mr. Ward should submit to an arrest within the territory of Massachusetts, and that the trial should be had before the court at Worcester, beyond the limits of the colony whose citizens were so generally embroiled in the question between their rival politicians.

The case appears to have excited no small interest, not only in Rhode Island, but also within the neighboring jurisdiction to which it was referred; and the distinguished name of James Otis is recorded as one of the counsel for the complainant. It would seem, however, that, after the virulence of party feeling had somewhat abated by the lapse of time, Mr. Hopkins attached less importance to a judicial remedy, and, it may be, felt less confidence in the justice of his cause; for, when the trial came on at Worcester, in 1759, he did not appear at the court, and, after his counsel had made some slight attempt to have the case continued to another term, it went against him by default, and he was required to pay the costs of the prosecution.

Thus ended a case of political litigation, in which, as usually happens in such transactions, the gratification of party feeling was the end proposed, far more than the vindication of injured justice. Mr. Ward does not appear to have been guilty of anything like slander, or even of reprehensible severity, in his remarks upon the administration of Mr. Hopkins, which were strictly confined to his official acts. Indeed, were such a writing to be produced in our own day, and aimed at a public officer on the eve of an election, it would rather be considered as remarkable for its courtesy and forbearance, and the candidate would be pronounced little less than mad, who, for no greater cause, should follow the example of Mr. Hopkins, and bring an action for slander against its author. But the adjudication of the suit pending between the rival chiefs of the Rhode Island parties by no means allayed the political strife with which the colony had already begun to be divided. Both Ward and Hopkins were now candidates for the office of Governor, and they continued to stand in opposition to each other, at the head of powerful parties, for nearly ten years, in which each experienced alternate success and defeat.

In the year 1761, Mr. Ward, having failed to secure an election to the chief magistracy, was appointed by the General Assembly to the office of Chief Justice of the colony, which, according to the charter, was an office of annual appointment. He discharged its duties with fidelity during the year for which he was appointed; but his position at the head of a party whose success was identified with his promotion (lid not allow him to remain in the quiet sphere of judicial life. He was the following year again summoned to the strife for executive office, and at the election in May, 1762, he was found to be the successful candidate, and was installed in the office of Governor. The struggle of the two parties is said to have been violent in the extreme, and the towns of the colony were nearly equally divided; those of the south generally voting for Mr. Ward, and those of the north, with few exceptions, being strongly in favor of Mr. Hopkins.

It was the ancient custom of the freeholders of Rhode Island, as the voters were then termed, to meet at Newport, at the general election in May of every year, and deposit, in person, their votes for the Governor, Assistants, and other general officers. In later periods it had been allowed, to those who could not attend the general election, to send their votes by those who went, and thus to deposit them by proxy; still, as the population of the several towns increased, an immense multitude would thus assemble from all parts of the colony, presenting a mass of human passions, which might be easily inflamed by the party excitements of the day, and which the sternest resolves of the government were sometimes unable to hold in check. The scene which was here presented, in a sharply contested election, would have furnished many attractive features for the satiric pencil of Hogarth. There were gathered all who were hoping for office, and all who were fearing to lose it; the leaders of either party exerting themselves, each to secure his own triumph, and the friends of each, confident of success, and eager for the result, discussing their respective merits with the loudest vociferations, and sometimes enforcing their opinions with fists and canes; and at length, when the vote was declared, and the proclamation made in the public square, according to the ancient custom, before all the people, the triumph of the successful party would go beyond all bounds of decency and order, and the day would sometimes end in disgraceful riot and confusion.

To prevent the recurrence of scenes like these, and also to save the time and expense that were wasted by this perilous gathering of the people, an important alteration was made in the election law in 1760. An act was passed by the legislature, providing that for the future the voting should be done by the citizens in their respective towns, and that none but members of the Assembly should be entitled to vote at Newport on the day of election. The passage of this law was most seasonable, and its results, in every way, were beneficial; the protracted controversy between the friends of Ward and of Hopkins had already begun, and, if the people had been still in the habit of assembling at Newport during its more exciting periods, the peace of the colony might have been seriously endangered in the party strifes that would have ensued.

The year during which Mr. Ward now held the office of Governor seems not to have been marked by any important public events. It deserves, however, to be mentioned, that during this period the project of founding an institution of learning in Rhode Island was first made a matter of serious interest and attention among the people. From the commencement of this important enterprise. Governor Ward took an active part in promoting its success. He belonged to that denomination of Christians by whom the idea was first proposed, and his own liberal tastes prompted him to give the full weight of his personal and official influence to the accomplishment of an undertaking fraught with so many blessings to the people of the colony.

He was present at the first meeting of gentlemen which was held to consider the expediency of the project. His name stands among the first of those who petitioned the legislature for the charter, and, when "Rhode Island College" was incorporated in 1764, he became one of the original trustees. This to him was no merely honorary post, but one that required of him a portion of his time and attention, which he freely gave to the interests of the infant institution. In 1767, he entered his son as a student in one of its earliest classes, and to the close of his life he continued its fast friend, as well as a member of its board of trustees.

Governor Ward's present term of office was a period of great suffering and anxiety among the tradesmen of the colony, in consequence of the extreme depreciation of the currency. The general scarcity of gold and silver, and the uncertain value of the colonial bills, depressed trade, and reduced especially the poorer classes of the people well-nigh to desperation. Murmurings and complaints arose from every quarter, and, notwithstanding the party then in power had always been known as the opponents of paper money, yet, in obedience to a natural propensity of the popular mind, strengthened perhaps, in this instance, by the intrigues of politicians, the evils of the time were very generally charged upon the administration; and, by means of the exertions which were made, the next election resulted in the defeat of Governor Ward, and the success of Governor Hopkins, who again took the oath of office in May, 1763.

At the close of his official year, Mr. Ward, who while he was Governor had resided at Newport, retired to his estate in Westerly, and, resuming the quiet occupations of the farmer and the trader, gave his time to the care of his family, to reading, and the society of his friends; a sphere of life in which he cultivated those elevated principles and amiable dispositions, which not all the rude collisions of politics, nor the agitations of a troubled age, were ever able to pervert or to change.

[1] For a full view of this curious subject, see a pamphlet by Elisha R. Potter, entitled "A Brief Account of Emissions of Paper Money made by the Colony of Rhode Island."

Chapter Four

The intervals which elapsed between the annual elections of general officers in Rhode Island seem to have passed quietly away, with but a rare collision of partisans, and only an occasional awakening of party feeling. But, as the political year drew to a close, and the season of general election came on, the whole colony became a scene of agitation and excitement. Every act that was performed, and every word that was uttered, by either of the candidates, became a matter of public interest, and, in the scarcity of newspapers, was repeated by political gossips in every place of public resort, and was borne to the fireside of every voter in the colony. Neighbor was arrayed against neighbor, and family against family, in an irreconcilable fend, which, unless it should be checked, threatened to ruin the peace of the community, and to be transmitted from father to son.

Impressed with the disastrous consequences of their wide separation from each other, the leading men of both parties seem, at different times, to have entertained plans of reconciliation, and of thus healing the wounds which had been made in the peace of the colony. The first distinct proposal, however, for this purpose, is believed to have come from Governor Ward, and is contained in the following letter, which he addressed to the General Assembly on the 28th of February, 1764, just as the arrangements for the annual election were about to be made.

"Gentlemen,

"The many ill consequences necessarily attending the division of the colony into parties are too manifest to require any enumeration, and call for the serious attention of every man who hath the welfare of his country at heart.

"Deeply affected with the melancholy prospect, and sincerely desirous to restore that peace and good order to the government, which have been too much obstructed, and without which we can never be extricated out of our present distressed situation, I beg leave to lay before you some proposals, which, in my humble opinion, might greatly tend to the accomplishment of these beneficial purposes.

"**1.** As the Honorable Stephen Hopkins, Esq., and myself, have been placed by our respective friends at the head of the two contending parties, I think it necessary, and accordingly propose, that both of us resign our pretensions to the chief seat of government; for the passions and prejudices of the people have been so warmly engaged for a long time against one or the other of us, that, should either Mr. Hopkins or myself be in the question, I imagine the spirit of party, instead of subsiding, would rage with as great violence as ever. And so greatly anxious am I for putting an end to those bitter heats and animosities, which have thrown the government into such confusion, that I can sincerely declare, that, for the sake of peace, I shall cheerfully resign all my pretensions to the office of Governor, or any other office.

"**2.** As it is clear and evident, for many reasons, that Newport is the most proper place for the residence of the Governor, I would propose that the Governor, to be elected upon this plan, should reside there, and the Deputy Governor in Providence.

"**3.** That the Upper House be equally divided between the two parties. This, I believe, would naturally tend to take away all pretence for a party.

"When I made proposals of this nature to Mr. Hopkins about two years ago, the principal objection that he made to them was, that a number of his friends had been deprived of offices, and no provision was made for restoring them. But as the case is since altered, and they are now restored, I hope every obstacle to the proposed plan is removed.

"That this may be the case, and that we may all heartily unite for the public good, is the sincere wish of. Gentlemen,

"Your most obedient humble servant,

"Samuel Ward."

On the same day, but apparently without any knowledge of the foregoing letter, the following proposition was made to Mr. Ward on the part of Governor Hopkins, viz.

"The death of the Honorable John Gardner, Esq., having left the place of Deputy-Governor vacant. Governor Hopkins, and those in the administration with him, invite and solicit the Honorable Samuel Ward, Esq., to accept of that office; hoping, as well as earnestly desiring, that such a measure carried into execution may put an end to the unhappy and destructive party disputes, which have too long been extremely injurious to the colony and its divided inhabitants.

" Stephen Hopkins, *Governor.*"

Such "were the proposals which were simultaneously made by each of the gentlemen who seemed to hold the peace of the colony in their hands. The terms in which they are both expressed, and the common spirit of apprehension which pervades them both, serve to indicate the fearful extent to which the party strife of the day had been carried. These proposals were respectively declined by each of the parties; Mr. Ward, it would appear from the correspondence, not thinking his acceptance of the post of Deputy-Governor likely to secure the peace of the community, and Mr. Hopkins regarding his surrender of the office of Governor as having no tendency to put an end to parties, but as evidently calculated to perpetuate them." As we review the correspondence which passed between them, and recur to the ordinary principles of human nature, it is not too much to suspect that an unwillingness to be second to a rival chief may have strengthened the conclusion of the one, and a reluctance to surrender the fascinating gift of political power may have stimulated the patriotism of the other. The attempts of both parties, however, proved abortive, and the contest went on with as much virulence of feeling as ever.

In May, 1765, Mr. Ward was again elected Governor of the colony, and went from Westerly to reside at Newport, where, in consequence of a re-election in the following year, he continued to reside till May, 1767. The two years during which he now held the chief magistracy were full of excitement, and were marked by events of high importance. A new spirit was rising in the minds of the colonists, and the petty distinctions of local party were for the time lost sight of in the deep indignation called forth by what were deemed the aggressions of the mother country on the rights of the colonies. In the preceding year the British ministry had already given intimations of their intention to tax America; and, soon after the election of Mr. Ward, the intelligence was received in Rhode Island, that the Stamp Act had passed both Houses of Parliament, and had received the royal approbation.

At one of the sessions of the previous year, the Colonial Assembly had given utterance to the feelings of their constituents, in the petition which they had adopted and sent to the King; and, though a considerable number of the wealthier inhabitants of Newport, and of some others of the southern towns, were still unwilling to oppose an act of Parliament, yet, no sooner was it known that the Stamp Act had become a law, than the minds of both the government and the people were made up to disregard its provisions. The act was not to go into operation till the following November, and the events of the interval only served to strengthen the determination to resist and to increase the irritability of the popular mind. Commissions were sent over, appointing the necessary officers to superintend the execution of the law, and the cruisers of the King, which seemed to multiply in all the ports of the colonies, became subjects of popular jealousy and hatred, on account of the closeness of their scrutiny, and the arrogance of their demands upon the inhabitants.

During the summer of 1765, while the *Maidstone* sloop of war was lying in the harbor of Newport, the captain, whose name was Charles Antrobus, impressed some sailors belonging to the town, and detained them on board his vessel. On a complaint being made. Governor Ward immediately wrote a request for their release, which not being complied with, a band of people at one of the wharves seized a boat belonging to the *Maidstone*, and burnt it in a public square. This act of violence gave rise to a series of retaliations on the part of the commander of the sloop, which for a time suspended all intercourse, and came near producing open hostilities between the people of the *Maidstone* and the inhabitants of the town. The Governor, in his correspondence with Captain Antrobus, contended, that "the impressing of Englishmen was an arbitrary action, contrary to law, inconsistent with liberty, and to be justified only by urgent necessity." "But, as the ship lay moored in an English colony, always ready to render any assistance necessary for his Majesty's service, there could be no possible reason sufficient to justify the severe and rigorous impress carried on in this port." He also firmly maintained the principle, that the commander and crew of a ship lying within the jurisdiction of the colony were subject to its laws.

The men, who had been impressed, were afterwards given up, but not till they had been detained for several weeks, during which there were frequent collisions between the people belonging to the vessel and the inhabitants of the town. Incidents like this served only to array the feelings of the colonists still more decidedly against the officers of the crown, and doubtless prepared the way for the excesses which were soon afterwards committed against the vindicators of the Stamp Act, and the officers who had been appointed to superintend its execution.

Mr. Augustus Johnson, a lawyer of respectable standing in Newport, had accepted the office of stamp master, in contempt alike of the arguments and the threatenings which were employed to dissuade him, and was preparing to perform its duties, when the day should arrive for the enforcement of the act. On the 27th of August, in open day, a few weeks after the affair of the *Maidstone*, a riotous collection of persons appeared in the streets of Newport, with a cart containing the effigies of Augustus Johnson, Martin Howard, and Dr. Thomas Moffat, the stamp master and two gentlemen who had written in defence of the act. each with a halter upon its neck. The images were drawn through the streets to a gallows which had been erected near the town house, and were there hung up till evening, to the gaze and derision of the multitude. On the following day the mob again assembled, and proceeded first to the house of Moffat, and afterwards to that of Howard, both of which they stripped of their furniture and nearly destroyed, the gentlemen themselves having escaped to a ship of war lying in the harbor. The house of Johnson was also assailed; but, by the persuasions of some of the principal men of the town, it was spared, on his giving a reluctant promise that he would not perform the duties of stamp master. [1]

Some efforts were made by the government of the colony to apprehend the persons who were engaged in these outrages, and the matter was soon after brought to the notice of the Assembly, by whom the Governor was requested to issue a proclamation commanding all officers to arrest the rioters wherever they might be found. But a similar scene had just before been enacted in Boston; and, in the excited state of the public mind which then prevailed, though most well-disposed people disapproved, and perhaps regretted the proceeding, yet none could be found who were willing to come forward and bear testimony against its authors.

The report of these outbreaks, which went home to England, produced upon the administration an impression most unfavorable to the reputation of the colony; and, in a letter which Governor Ward soon afterwards received from the agent in London, it was stated that the Lords of the Treasury had determined to withhold the money which was still due to the colon}^ for the supplies she had furnished in the war, until full indemnification should be made to those who had suffered from the proceedings of the rioters. This information gave rise to a long correspondence between the government of the colony and the Secretary of State in England. in which the claim of Rhode Island to compensation was urged on independent grounds; but the condition was still insisted on, and the money was withheld by the ministry. [2] Several attempts were subsequently made to get a bill through the Assembly to indemnify the stamp master and his associates, who had suffered at Newport, but in every instance without success; and, as no restitution appears ever to have been made, it is presumed that the services of the colony remained unrequited, until the revolution put an end to all urging of the claim. [3]

While these events were in progress, the Stamp Act was becoming a still more engrossing subject of popular attention; and, as the time for its enforcement approached, the feelings of the community were raised to the highest pitch of excitement. The association of the *Sons of Liberty*, who pledged themselves to abstain from the use of every article bearing the odious stamp, extended throughout the colony. Many of the towns held meetings, and instructed their deputies to urge the strongest measures in opposition to the act; and

the Assembly, at its session in September, adopted the five celebrated resolutions which had been drawn up by Patrick Henry, four
of which had just before been passed by the House of Burgesses of
Virginia. The fourth resolution received an important modification
by the omission of the words "his Majesty or his substitutes," and,
as adopted by the Assembly, declared that their own body possessed "the only exclusive right to lay taxes and imposts upon the
inhabitants of the colony." To these resolutions they also added another, breathing the spirit of a still bolder opposition to the aggressions of the ministry, in which they directed all the officers appointed by the authority of the colony "to proceed in the execution
of their respective offices in the same manner as usual, and that
this Assembly will indemnify and save harmless all the said officers
on account of their conduct, agreeable to this resolution." These
resolutions, taken as a whole, are nearly equivalent to a declaration
of independence, though no formal act of the kind had then been
proposed. They appear to have been, at the time of their adoption,
decidedly in advance of those of any other colony, in the tone of
resolute independence which pervades them, and were undoubtedly a true expression of the general feeling which reigned among the
people.

At the same session the Assembly also appointed delegates to
the Colonial Congress, which was soon to meet at New York, for the
purpose of representing to his Majesty the views entertained by the
people of America respecting the Stamp Act. The gentlemen selected for this delegation were Henry Ward, a younger brother of the
Governor, and Metcalf Bowles, both of them citizens of eminent
standing, and holding high offices in the colony. The instructions
which the Assembly voted to the delegates breathed the same determined spirit as the resolutions to which we have already referred, and evinced, in the most unequivocal manner, that they regarded the concerns committed to the Congress as "of the last consequence to themselves, to their constituents, and to posterity."

In the spring of the year 1767, the hostility subsisting between
the political parties of the colony reappeared in all its violence. Mr.
Hopkins was again the opposing candidate for the office of Governor, at the head of a ticket of general officers, who, with reference
to the distracted condition of the community, were styled by their
friends *Seekers of Peace*. The contest which ensued was attended

with unusual excitement in every part of the colony; the towns north of Bristol and Warwick all giving large majorities for Hopkins, while the southern towns gave their votes, with scarcely less unanimity, for Ward. The campaign resulted in the election of Mr. Hopkins by a larger majority than he had ever before received.

This election was the last in which these gentlemen appeared as candidates in opposition to each other. At the meeting of the Assembly in the following March, the season at which the arrangements for the annual election were usually made, Governor Hopkins, who had been elected as a *peace-maker*, in behalf of himself and the friends who supported him, put forth substantially the same proposals for the pacification of the colony, which Mr. Ward had made four years before, and which he had then rejected. These were, that both the rival candidates should relinquish all pretensions to the chief place in the government, and that the two parties should unite in forming an administration, in which one should nominate a Governor, and the other a Deputy-Governor, each from the ranks of its own opponents. The terms were readily accepted by Governor Ward and his friends; and the two chiefs, who had so long been arrayed in opposition to each other, met first at Providence, and afterwards at Newport, and settled the preliminaries of what proved to be a lasting and happy coalition.

Thus ended what perhaps deserves to be regarded as the most remarkable contest of parties which has occurred in the history of Rhode Island. The inquirer at this distant day, who explores its half-forgotten records, finds but little to explain the length to which it was protracted, or the acrimony with which it was carried on. Though it was occasionally involved with questions of public policy, yet, in the main, it seems not to have depended on any important principle of government, or any leading interest of society. It was a warfare between men and classes, and not between measures and interests. The gentlemen, who for nearly ten years stood at the head of the respective parties, were both persons of liberal minds, and, it would seem, were quite above the petty ambition, which seeks office merely for the sake of its trifling rewards; and the strife in which they were so long and so warmly engaged can only be accounted for by referring it to the natural antagonism, which, in certain states of society, always exists between persons of different classes, and different occupations and habits of life. The portion of the community who supported Governor Ward regarded themselves as the most suitable guardians of the public weal, on account of their hereditary wealth, their intelligence, and their elevated position in society; while those who favored Governor Hopkins were perhaps at first thrown into the opposition by their jealousy of a class who claimed to be their superiors in social importance, and who had long been accustomed to wield the political power of the colony.

The continuance of the controversy had been productive of unnumbered evils, and, on account of the expense and the excitement it occasioned, had doubtless become wearisome to the leading members of both parties. Besides, other questions had arisen, embracing wilder interests than those of a single colony, and new parties were already forming on principles which involved the dearest rights of Englishmen. Before these higher questions, the petty strifes of local politics necessarily lost their importance, and the spirit which had hitherto animated them became speedily merged in patriotic solicitude for the liberties of the country.

[1] See *Life of Augustus Johnson,* in Updike's *Memoirs of the Rhode Island Bar*, p. 67. Mr. Updike represents the riot as having occurred in 1766, after the repeal of the Stamp Act; but the recorded proceedings of the legislature, and a notice in the *Providence Gazette*, fix it in 1765.

[2] Two letters relating to this subject, addressed by Governor Ward, one to Mr. Secretary Conway, and the other to the Earl of Shelburne, are contained in Almon's *Prior Documents,* pp. 102 and 118.

[3] A bill passed the House of Assistants, in 1768, making full indemnification for the losses of property sustained by these men; but the claims which they presented were deemed exorbitant by the Lower House, and were also without satisfactory certificates; they were accordingly dismissed. In 1772, the claims were again before the Assembly, and reexamined by a committee appointed for the purpose. After undergoing considerable reduction by the committee, they were at length allowed by both Houses, and were ordered to be paid when the Lords of the Treasury should pay the debt due to the colony for its services in the war. This was never paid.

Chapter Five

Previously to the period at which Governor Ward closed his official connection with the government of the colony, we have seen that he was more than once called, in the discharge of his duty, to take a firm stand against the encroachments which the ministry had already commenced upon the rights of the colonists. To the position which he thus assumed, we have every reason to believe, he was directed not less by his personal convictions than by the dictates of official duty. From the beginning of the contest with the mother country, he seems to have given his whole influence to the colonial side of the questions at issue; and, as he was at the head of the party then in power, he was doubtless largely instrumental in promoting the unanimity of feeling, which characterized the opposition to the Stamp Act in the colony, after the repeal of this act, however, and the passage of the revenue laws of 1767 and 1769, the issue which was presented was thought to be different from that of former years, and many of the wealthy merchants of Newport, and of other towns of Rhode Island, who had acted with Governor Ward in all the contests of local politics, were now willing to engage but feebly, if at all, in measures of resistance to the authority of Parliament.

To him, however, the questions which were presented were still the same, and his views of their importance to the colonies, or of the measures which it was necessary to adopt in opposing them, were not changed by the opinions of his former friends and supporters. He was now in private life; but he still watched with anxious interest the course of public events, and, through the medium of his correspondence, and of occasional intercourse with the leading patriots of New England, hc contributed the influence of his own earnest views towards forming the public sentiment that ruled the events of the time.

After the renewal of the attempt to tax the colonies by the Townshend administration, the coast of New England was carefully watched by cruisers employed by the commissioners of customs, to repress the illegal traffic which was extensively carried on, and to aid the customhouse officers in enforcing the laws for collecting the revenue. For these vessels, the harbor of Newport was one of the principal rendezvous, and, being an important port of entry, it was constantly frequented by them. The harsh impressments, and the arrogant demands for supplies which were often made by their commanders, gave rise to frequent collisions between them and the inhabitants of the colony, and tended gradually to detach from the mother country the affections even of those who had hitherto taken no part in the resistance which had been made to the acts of Parliament. These insolent displays of authority, and the annoyances which were suffered in consequence in many parts of the colony, seem to have rendered the minds of the people peculiarly irritable, and, like the presence of troops among the inhabitants of Boston, to have kept alive a hostile feeling, which any slight occasion was sufficient to fan into a flame.

Such an occasion was presented in the summer of the year 1769. The armed sloop *Liberty*, commanded by Captain Reid, brought into the harbor of Newport two vessels, one a sloop, and the other a brig, which she had taken in Long Island Sound, on suspicion of their being engaged in the contraband traffic. The sloop appears to have been open to suspicion, but the brig had regularly cleared at the custom-house of the port from which she sailed. Both of them, however, were forcibly detained beneath the guns of the cruiser, and occupied by a guard whom Captain Reid had placed on board. The seizure was thought to be illegal by the people of the town, and their sympathies were warmly enlisted in behalf of the captured vessels. The commander of the brig, on finding himself thus stripped of his command, and even refused access to his personal wardrobe, was forced into an altercation and scuffle with the man who had been set over him, and afterwards, while passing to the shore in his boat, was fired upon by the crew of the *Liberty*. This was provocation enough to call forth all the indignant feeling which had long existed in the popular mind towards the cruisers of the King. The captain of the *Liberty*, being found on shore on the evening of the same day, was seized by the people, and compelled to send for his crew, in order that the person who had fired upon the captain of the brig might be identified. In the meantime, a party from the shore went off to the sloop, cut the cables which moored her, and, on her drifting to a neighboring pointy dismantled her, and a few days afterwards burnt her to the water's edge. [1]

This destruction of the sloop *Liberty*, in the harbor of Newport, has been justly claimed as among the earliest, in point of time, of the acts of open resistance to British power, which terminated in the final separation of the colonies from England. It was followed, three years later, by the destruction of the schooner *Gaspee*, upon the waters of the same bay, and within the jurisdiction of the same colony; and, though less important from the consequences it produced, yet, as an illustration of the spirit of the colony, it deserves a place in the history of the revolutionary struggle, on the same page which records that famous achievement. Immediately after the attack upon the *Liberty*, the Governor, with the advice of such of the assistants as he could assemble, issued a proclamation, directing the officers of the King "to use their utmost endeavors to inquire after and discover" the persons engaged in the riot, and the commissioners of customs published a notice offering a reward of a hundred pounds for any information which should lead to their detection. But no judicial investigation was ever held, and neither the proclamation made by the Governor, nor the reward offered by the commissioners, in the state of feeling then prevalent in the colony, was sufficient to elicit any important evidence.

The destruction of the *Gaspee*, in addition to the numerous acts of resistance which had preceded it, created in the minds of the ministry the deepest dislike towards the colony, and a determination to humble its spirit by every means in their power. It is said they formed the purpose of quartering some regiments of soldiers in its two principal towns, and even advised the King to abrogate the charter, which had been granted by Charles the Second. For the purpose of investigating the circumstances attending the burning of the schooner, a court of commissioners was appointed under the authority of the great seal, with instructions to employ, if necessary, the troops of the King in executing their commission, and to deliver the persons, who should be found to have participated in the affair, to the commander of one of the ships of war, to be transported to England for trial. The extraordinary powers and arbitrary proceedings of this high court of inquiry were subjects of widespread apprehension, and attracted the attention of the House of Burgesses of Virginia, who appointed a committee to inquire into their bearing upon the rights and liberties of the colonies. The investigations of this court, however, which were conducted with great assiduity for many weeks, were at length brought to a close, without leading to the detection of any of the offenders, notwithstanding the fact that they were well known to hundreds of the people of the colony.

The incidents, which we have thus related, illustrate the state of popular feeling in Rhode Island, in the early stages of the contest with Great Britain. That these acts of violence were illegal, and against the peace and good order of the colony, cannot be denied; and as such they seem to have been generally regarded at the time. But, when viewed in their connection with the revolutionary struggle, which was already commencing, they are not to be condemned as crimes against society. They were rather the natural consequences of the injurious laws of Parliament, and especially of the oppressive manner in which those laws were executed by the officers of the King, who were sent to the colony.

These officers were in the habit not only of searching every vessel that came within their reach, which sometimes occasioned a detention of several days, but they would often seize upon the market boats which plied upon the bay, for the trifling purpose of examining the freights which they contained, and would subject their crews, who were usually farmers from the country, to every species of indignity and oppression. They seldom took the trouble to exhibit their commissions to any of the magistrates of the colony, but seemed to hold themselves above the laws, and to sport with the interests and rights of the inhabitants. As they were perpetually hovering upon the coast, and seldom remained long in port, legal redress for the injuries they occasioned was impossible; and it is not strange that they should have occasionally experienced the vengeance of an insulted people.

The sky was now growing dark with clouds that portended still more violent commotions. The impression which had been produced by the destruction of the *Gaspee*, and by the proceedings of the commissioners who were appointed to inquire into the affair, instead of humbling the spirit of the colony, as was intended, served only to prepare the minds of the people for still further acts of resistance. Reverence for the authority of Parliament was rapidly passing away, and the necessity of boldly withstanding the enforcement of the revenue acts was every day becoming more apparent. Agreements of non-importation and non-consumption had been formed among the inhabitants of Newport and Providence, as early as 1769; and, though they seem not in all cases to have been very faithfully adhered to, yet they served to organize the opposition that was now very generally felt towards the proceedings of Parliament.

The tax on tea was still continued; and the unusual facilities for its importation into the colonies, which had been granted to the East India Company, created among the people, especially of the commercial towns, an apprehension that they might at length be obliged to submit to the tyranny that threatened them. In this apprehension Rhode Island largely shared; for she presented the most accessible port upon the coast, and numbered among her eminent merchants a few, at least, who might have consented to act as factors of the Company, for the sale of the tea.

During the whole period through which we have thus traced the early progress of the revolutionary contest in Rhode Island, Governor Ward had lived in comparative retirement upon his estate at Westerly. He was here surrounded by his numerous family, and by an extensive circle of friends. He had not been exempt from the melancholy changes incident to every human lot, but had buried several of his kindred and his dearest friends; and, though he had lost none of his children, he had been stricken with a still heavier calamity in the loss of his wife, the amiable and worthy companion of many years, who died in December, 1770. In addition to the care of his family, and the management of his estate, his attention had been in part occupied by a vexatious suit at law with a troublesome neighbor, in which he had been compelled to engage, in vindication of his title to a tract of land lying in the Narragansett country. The suit was at length decided in his favor, after being protracted through several years, during which his opponent attempted to enlist against him the partisan feeling which still survived the controversy in which he had formerly been engaged.

But he was also a close observer of the course of public events; and, though dwelling apart from the excited feeling which now pervaded the larger towns, he was not the less informed of the progress of liberal sentiments, or the less able to estimate with calm judgment the magnitude of the issues to which they were leading. It was his habit frequently to attend the sessions of the General Assembly, and, though he held no official connection with the government, his position in the colony enabled him to exert a wide influence upon the popular mind, and rendered his advice and sanction exceedingly important in the decision of every question of great public interest.

Thus far in the contest, the opposition, which had manifested itself to the measures of the ministry in the several colonies, had resulted from accidental causes, rather than from any concerted plan, which had been agreed upon for the purpose. The state of the question, however, had now become such, that some arrangement for circulating important intelligence, and for promoting unity of action, was absolutely essential. For this purpose, the House of Burgesses of Virginia, on the 12th of March, 1773, appointed a standing committee of correspondence and inquiry, whose duty it should be to obtain the earliest intelligence of all measures of the British government relating to America, and to maintain a correspondence with such committees as should be appointed for a similar purpose by the other colonies, to whom the adoption of the measure was earnestly recommended. The recommendation of Virginia was immediately adopted by the Assembly of Rhode Island at its session in the following May, and seven of the leading citizens of the colony were appointed a committee of correspondence, one of whom was Mr. Henry Ward, a younger brother of the Governor, at that time holding the office of Secretary of State.

From this period the colony of Rhode Island was among the foremost in activity and zeal, both in devising and executing measures for the promotion of the common cause. Soon after these arrangements had been adopted for securing a greater unity of sentiment and of action among the colonies, the shipment of several cargoes of tea was made by the East India Company to some of the American ports, and serious apprehensions were entertained by many of the friends of liberty in Rhode Island, that boxes of the obnoxious article might be clandestinely entered at Newport. In order to provide against such an occurrence, and to secure a more perfect organization throughout the colony. Governor Ward, in December, 1773, a few days after the destruction of the tea at Boston, addressed a letter, signed by himself and several others of the inhabitants of Westerly, to some of the leading gentlemen of Newport, urging the establishment of a committee of correspondence in each of the towns of the colony, and suggesting that Newport, as the seat of the government and the emporium of trade, should take the lead in carrying forward the measure.

This letter, which breathes the spirit of a cautious and wise man, who clearly saw the storm that was gathering over the colonies, was submitted to the people of Newport at a town meeting; and the suggestions it contained were soon afterwards adopted, and carried into effect. He also addressed similar letters to leading men in other towns of the colony; and early in February, 1774, having himself accepted the post of chairman of the committee of correspondence of the town of Westerly, he introduced a series of resolutions, at a meeting of the town, which, taken as a whole, form a complete embodiment of the principles maintained by the colonies, and of the grounds upon which they rest. For the purpose, as is probable, of instructing the citizens of the town respecting the cause in which they were embarked, the resolutions recited very fully the grievances which were complained of, and earnestly, yet calmly, urged resistance as the only remedy which was left, and as a high civic duty, which they owed not less to themselves, than to the whole British empire and to posterity.

[1] See Staples's *Gaspee Documents*; and, for a fuller account of the affair, Bull's *Memoir of the Colony*, for 1769.

Chapter Six

The English ministry had already become thoroughly incensed at the spirit which the colonies, especially Massachusetts Bay, had constantly evinced towards all their measures for raising a revenue in America; and, on receiving intelligence of the destruction of the tea at Boston, they immediately determined to avenge the insult, which had been offered to their authority. Accordingly, within a month after the intelligence was received at London, they carried through Parliament, by a large majority, the three celebrated bills, known as the Boston Port bill, the bill for the better regulating of the government of Massachusetts Bay, and the bill for removing persons accused of certain offences to another colony, or to England, for trial. These famous bills were regarded as special acts of ministerial vengeance, and the alarm which they everywhere occasioned formed one of the most powerful of the agencies which hastened forward the crisis of the revolution. Instead of the olive branch which many had hoped to see, the colonists now saw that only a naked sword was held out to them.

The sufferings of the people of Boston became a subject of universal sympathy, and a general Congress of delegates from all the colonies soon began to be talked of. The first distinct proposal of such a Congress, however, by any public body, it is believed, was made by the town of Providence, at a meeting held on the 17th of May, 1774. At this meeting, the deputies of the town were instructed "to use their influence at the approaching session of the General Assembly of this colony, for promoting a Congress, as soon as may be, of the representatives of the General Assemblies of the several colonies and provinces of North America, for promoting the firmest union, and adopting such measures as to them shall appear the most effectual to answer that important purpose, and to agree upon proper methods of executing the same." [1] The citizens of Providence, at the same meeting, also directed the committee of correspondence to assure the people of Boston of the sympathy they felt for the distressed condition of that town, and that they regarded their cause as the common cause of the whole country.

The session of the General Assembly was held at Newport on the second Monday in June: and, though none of the other colonies had at this time taken any formal action respecting the proposed Congress, yet the spirit of its members was already prepared to respond to the instructions of the deputies from Providence. The subject was taken up at the beginning of the session, and, after mature consideration, the Assembly, on the 15th of June, adopted a series of resolutions setting forth the condition of the colonies, and declaring that a convention of representatives from them all ought to be holden as soon as practicable. By the same resolutions, Stephen Hopkins and Samuel Ward were appointed to represent the colony, and were specially directed "to endeavor to procure a regular annual convention of representatives from all the colonies." In this vote, which was adopted with great unanimity, all party feuds were buried for ever; and the political leaders, who, in former years, had so often been arrayed against each other, were henceforth to be united as friends and fellow-patriots in the council that planned the revolution. In this council their appointment bore the earliest date among those of all its 'members; and, until separated by death, it is believed, they shared each other's confidence and sympathy in all the arduous duties in which they were engaged. [2]

The views, with which Mr. Ward accepted the important trust that was now committed to him, were of the gravest and most serious character. He was no frantic patriot, who supposed that vaporing resolutions and exciting speeches were all that was needed for the crisis which he saw was approaching. A large acquaintance with human nature made him distrust the hope, which many entertained, that the determinations of the ministry would be changed by any remonstrances or threatenings of the colonies; and the religious sentiments which he had early imbibed, and which were now woven into all his reflections, imparted a deeply moral aspect to all the questions which were likely to be presented to the body to which he had been appointed. But he had already decided on which side the right certainly lay, and he did not waver from the decision to which he had come. In a letter to his brother, written in the following year, but referring to this period, he says of himself,

"When I first entered this contest with Great Britain, I extended my views through the various scenes which my judgment, or imagination, (say which you please,) pointed out to me. I saw clearly, that the last act of this cruel tragedy would close in fields of blood. I have traced the progress of this unnatural war through burning towns, devastation of the country, and every subsequent evil. I have realized, with regard to myself, the bullet, the bayonet, and the halter; and, compared with the immense object I have in view, they are all less than nothing. No man living, perhaps, is more fond of his children than I am, and I am not so old as to be tired of life; and yet, as far as I can now judge, the tenderest connections and the most important private concerns are very minute objects. Heaven save my country, I was going to say, is my first, my last, and almost my only prayer."

The delegates of the several colonies were at length all chosen, and the place was fixed upon at which the Congress should assemble. Mr. Ward left his home about the middle of August, attended by a faithful family servant, and arrived at the place of meeting on the 30th of the same month. The journey was made on horseback, and, on the day after his arrival, he acknowledged, with pious gratitude, in a letter addressed to his children, the kind Providence which had watched over him amidst the perils of the way. On the morning of the 5th of September, 1774, the "Old Congress," as it is now familiarly known in our history, commenced its sessions, in Carpenters Hall, in Philadelphia. The place but ill corresponded with the real magnitude of the occasion. No tapestry bedecked its walls, no images of sages and heroes of other days looked down upon the scene. Yet, to one who could read the future, it would have presented a simple grandeur, such as we may now look for in vain within the majestic halls of the Capitol, and amidst the imposing forms of the constitution.

The forty-four individuals, who met on that day for the first time, were men of different characters and different opinions, for they had come from the extremes of the continent; but they came together unfettered by partisan or sectional feeling. The simple (Quakers of Pennsylvania, the high-spirited Cavaliers of Virginia and Carolina, and the resolute Puritans of Massachusetts and Connecticut, all were represented in that body of grave and earnest-minded men; yet, amidst all differences of temperament, of creed, and of opinion, the pervading sentiment was catholic and patriotic. They had been roused from the repose of their homes by common grievances, and they only sought a common redress.

Their resolution of secrecy, the first which they adopted after their organization, was so sacredly kept, that a veil has rested upon their proceedings to this day, which even the publication of their Secret Journal has aided us but little in removing. But tradition has reported the eloquence of their debates, and the recorded results which they achieved fully show that their daily sessions were seasons of unremitted deliberation upon the questions before them. Among the different classes of measures which were proposed to the Congress, Mr. Ward, if we may judge from the occasional allusions in his correspondence, was always an advocate of the moderate counsels which so eminently characterize its published documents. Cooler and more quiet in his temperament than some others of the New England delegates, while he regarded a separation from the mother country as sooner or later inevitable, he was still in favor of first trying every pacific measure, and of thus placing the cause in the best possible light, both before the colonies and the world.

The Congress closed its session on the 26th of October, after appointing another session to be held on the 10th day of the following May, unless the public grievances should be removed before that time. The results of its six weeks' deliberation were then probably but imperfectly comprehended, even by those of its members who looked farthest into the vista of the future. The consultations which were held, and the friendships which were formed, blending with the common interests and common dangers of the whole country, became enduring bonds of union to the colonies, which no subsequent differences of opinion, nor all the gloomy disasters of the revolution, were able to break asunder.

The delegates from Rhode Island returned immediately to their homes; and at a meeting of the General Assembly, called specially for the purpose, they made a full report of the proceedings of the Congress. Its several acts were unanimously approved, and the delegates, having received the thanks of the Assembly, were immediately appointed to attend the next Congress, and charged with suitable instructions as to the objects to be accomplished.

Before the meeting of the second Congress, the fields of Lexington had been reddened with blood, spilt in the earliest engagement of the revolution. Tidings of the battle were received in Rhode Island on the evening: of the 19th of April, and companies from the northern towns of the colony made immediate preparation to march to the assistance of the people of Massachusetts. On the 22d of the same month, a special session of the Assembly was held at Providence, and acts were passed for putting the colony in a posture of defence, and for raising fifteen hundred men, to act with similar quotas from Massachusetts and Connecticut, as an army of observation. At the same session, Nathaniel Greene was advanced from the station of a private in the Kentish Guards, the company of his native town, to the rank of Brigadier-General, and was placed at the head of the troops from Rhode Island.

To these spirited proceedings of the Assembly, the Governor, Mr. Joseph Wanton, and the Deputy-Governor, and several of the Assistants, entered a formal protest, on the ground that they were unnecessary, and might still further disturb the relations of the colonies with the mother country. But, in an emergency like this, the protest of men who had been intrusted with the government of the colony was not to be endured by the people. So high was the excitement among the members of the Assembly, that the Deputy-Governor and the recreant Assistants were obliged to resign their places; and the Governor, though he had just before been elected for another term, was suspended from the exercise of all official authority. A few months afterwards, the office was taken from Mr. Wanton by an act of the Assembly, and bestowed upon Mr. Nicolas Cooke, an eminent merchant of Providence, who held it with dignity and firmness for three successive years, during the most trying period of the revolution.

In this disordered state of the colonial government, the delegates from Rhode Island again departed to join the Congress at Philadelphia. Their credentials bore only the signature of Henry Ward, Secretary of State, whom the legislature, on account of the defection of the Governor and his Deputy, had authorized to sign the public papers of the colony. Mr. Ward appeared and took his seat on the 15th of May, five days after the session began. The papers relating to the battle of Lexington had already been presented by Mr. Hancock, on the first day of the session; and, in promoting the measures which were now proposed for the defence of the colonies, and for raising and equipping troops, he engaged with the utmost zeal. His son, Samuel Ward, Junior, who had been recently graduated at Rhode Island College, had just received a captain's commission in the service of his native colony; and this circumstance, in connection with the views which he had long taken of the nature of the contest, and the necessity of preparing for the worst, may have strengthened his interest in the military establishment of the country. In carrying forward all these measures, Mr. Ward earnestly cooperated with John Adams, the farsighted leader of the New England delegations, who at this very time was writing those delightful Letters, which now throw so much light upon the deliberations which were held at Philadelphia.

On the 26th of May, when the House resolved itself into a committee of the whole, "on the consideration of the state of America," Mr. Ward was called to the chair by Mr. Hancock, who had then just been elected President; and from this time onwards he seems to have been selected to preside in the committee of the whole, whenever the Congress gave this form to its deliberations. In this situation he was, of course, precluded from engaging in the debates of the committee; but, on the questions which were discussed in the

House itself, he was accustomed to deliver his sentiments with manly clearness and earnest eloquence. Every day's deliberations only served to unite the minds of all the delegates in the opinion, which a few had entertained from the beginning, that a reconciliation was not to be expected, and that vigorous measures must immediately be adopted for defence and resistance. This sentiment is everywhere expressed in the letters of Mr. Ward, written, at this period, to his friends in Rhode Island, and to his kinsman General Greene, and his son Captain Ward, at the camp before Boston. With these and some other officers in active service he maintained a frequent correspondence, that he might the better ascertain the views of the troops, and judge of the public measures needed for their discipline and efficiency.

General Greene, on the 4th of June, writes to him his opinion, that all the forces in America should be under one commander, raised and appointed by the same authority, subjected to the same regulations, and ready to be detached wherever occasion may require;" [3] and on the 15th of the same month, we find in the Journal of Congress the following entry;

"Agreeable to order, the Congress resolved itself into a committee of the whole, and, after some time, the President resumed the chair, and Mr. Ward reported that the committee had come to further resolutions, which he was ordered to report. It was then resolved, That a General be appointed to command all the Continental forces raised, or to be raised, for the defence of American liberty.

"The Congress then proceeded to the choice of a General by ballot, and George Washington. Esq., was unanimously elected."

Though the full importance of the step which was now taken could not then have been realized, yet there were those who saw clearly that they had staked the destiny of the colonies upon the election which they had made. Mr. Ward had formed the acquaintance of Washington in the session of the preceding year, and appears immediately to have conceived for him that sentiment of mingled reverence and esteem, which his character never failed to inspire in every ingenuous mind. The vote which was adopted a few days after the election, and which pledged the delegates to maintain and assist the Commander-in-chief with their lives and fortunes, was on his part a pledge of the deepest and sincerest devotion. A month or two later, in a letter written to the General in the hurry of public business, he says, "I most cheerfully entered upon a solemn engagement, upon your appointment, to support you with my life and my fortune; and I shall most religiously, and with the highest pleasure, endeavor to discharge that duty."

In August, 1775, the Congress took a recess for a month, and Mr. Ward passed the interval with his family in Rhode Island. During this period he also attended the meeting of the General Assembly, and, in connection with his colleague, Mr. Hopkins, made a report to that body of the condition of the colonies, and the measures which had been adopted for their common safety. He found the people of Rhode Island, though still animated with the same devotion to liberty, yet more than usually distressed at the depredations of the ships of war which now covered the Narragansett Bay, and frequently sent their tenders marauding along its shores. A large proportion of the towns of the colony border upon navigable waters, and the property of their citizens was thus continually exposed to the incursions of an enemy, who had full possession of the harbor of Newport, and withal was not without the confidence of some of the leading citizens of the town.

The great body of the people, however, had long since espoused the American cause, though, as their fidelity had been put to severer tests than that of most other towns, it had not wholly escaped suspicion. The commerce, which had hitherto supported the town, within a single year had been reduced to less than a third of its former extent, and the sources of its long-continued prosperity were rapidly drying up. Mr. Ward, whose sympathies were warmly enlisted in the sufferings of his native town, foreseeing the doom that must descend upon it when hostilities should assume a still sterner aspect, earnestly advised its inhabitants, who were true to the country, to remove their families and effects to other parts of the colony. The people of Providence also offered to make provision for the reception and support of some hundreds of the poor families of Newport. The proposal, however, seems not at the time to have been generally accepted; and the long possession of the British, and the melancholy desolations of war, annihilated the prosperity of the town, and at the close of the revolution left nothing of her former glory, save the changeless beauties of nature which surround her.

For the purpose of protecting the trade of the colony, the General Assembly, in June, 1775, chartered and equipped two vessels of considerable force, and placed them under the command of Abraham Whipple, to whom was given the title of Commodore. He also received private instructions to clear the bay of the tenders of the British frigate *Rose*, that lay at its mouth; and in his first cruise, after a slight engagement, the first concerted naval engagement of the revolution, he captured one of the tenders, and brought her to Providence. In August this armament was increased by the addition of two row galleys, carrying thirty men each; and, on the 26th of that month, the General Assembly adopted a resolution, instructing the delegates of the colony "to use their whole influence, at the ensuing Congress, for building, at the Continental expense, a fleet of sufficient force for the protection of these colonies, and for employing it in such manner and places, as will most effectually annoy our enemies, and contribute to the common defence of these colonies." [4]

This resolution was the earliest proposal for a Continental navy. It was the natural result of the maritime experience of the colony, and of the several encounters of her citizens with the cruisers of the King. The annoyances, which they had thus experienced, enabled them to appreciate the advantages which might be derived from a naval armament, and their familiarity with the sea led them earnestly to engage in its establishment.

These instructions were presented to the Congress on the 3d day of October, and were ordered to lie upon the table. Several vessels of different force were soon afterwards either built or chartered for the service of the colonies, and Esek Hopkins, at that time a Brigadier-General in the army of Rhode Island, was appointed to the command of the infant navy. He repaired to Philadelphia immediately on receiving his appointment, in November, 1775, and in the following February sailed with the entire fleet on an expedition against one of the Bermuda Islands. The expedition seems to have been undertaken without any precise orders from the Congress, and, though in some respects eminently successful, it failed to receive their entire sanction.

In consequence of the urgency of other business, the instructions to the delegates of Rhode Island were not taken up for the action of the House till the 16th of November, though several of the intervening days had been assigned for their consideration. On this day Mr. Ward wrote to his brother in Rhode Island, "Our instruction for an American fleet has been long upon the table. When it was first presented, it was looked upon as perfectly chimerical; but gentlemen now consider it in a very different light. It is this day to be taken into consideration, and I have great hopes of carrying it. Dr. Franklin and Colonel Lee, the two Adamses, and many others, will support it. If it succeeds, I shall remember your ideas of our building two of the ships." The matter, however, seems not to have been brought to a final determination till the 11th of December; for in the Journal we find the following entry for that day;

"Agreeable to the order of the day. the Congress took into consideration the instructions given to the delegates of Rhode Island, and after debate thereon, Resolved, That a committee be appointed to devise ways and means for furnishing these colonies with a naval armament, and report with all convenient speed."

This committee brought in their report on the 13th of December, and recommended that thirteen ships, five of thirty-two guns, five of twenty-eight guns, and three of twenty-four guns, be built and made ready for sea as soon as practicable. The report of the committee, after being fully debated, was adopted by the Congress, and the ships were ordered to be built at the expense of the united colonies. On the day following the final adoption of this measure, Mr. Ward again wrote to his brother, "I have the pleasure to acquaint you, that, upon considering our instructions for a navy, the Congress has agreed to build thirteen ships of war. A committee is to be this day appointed, with full powers to carry the resolve into execution. Powder and duck are ordered to be imported. All other articles, it is supposed, may be got in the colonies. Two of these vessels are to be built in our colony, one in New Hampshire, &c. The particulars I would not have mentioned. The ships are to be built with all possible despatch."

We have thus seen that the first establishment of a Continental fleet is to be traced back to the instructions of the Rhode Island Assembly, and to the exertions which were made in obedience to them by the delegates of the colony. The measure was on every account an important one, and the merit of originating and supporting it, at that opening period of the struggle for independence, ought not to be lightly estimated. It is alone sufficient to entitle the colony to an honorable distinction in the history of the revolution, and may be regarded as the early pledge of the brilliant deeds, which have since been achieved by her sons upon the decks of the American navy.

[1] Staples's *Annals of Providence*, p. 235. This date is four days earlier than the action of any other public body on the subject.

[2] The delegates from Massachusetts were appointed on the 17th of June, which has generally, though erroneously, been considered as the date of the earliest appointment. So far as is now known, it was at a Rhode Island town meeting that the first public proposal of a Congress was made, and at a session of the Rhode Island Assembly, that the first delegates to that Congress were appointed.

[3] The same letter contains the following, at that time, remarkable passage; "Permit me, then, to recommend, from the sincerity of my heart, ready at all times to bleed in my country's cause, a declaration of independence; and a call upon the world, and the great God who governs it, to witness the necessity, propriety, and rectitude thereof."

[4] Staples's *Annals of Providence,* p. 265; also *Schedules of the General Assembly of Rhode Island.*

Chapter Seven

In the Journals of the Continental Congress for the session of 1775, and the early part of the following year, few names, after those of the immediate leaders of the revolution, are more frequently mentioned than that of Samuel Ward. Though not unused to debate, it is probable that his most important services were performed in a less conspicuous sphere of action. Indeed the real work of such bodies is usually accomplished away from the scenes of brilliant oratory, in the confinement of the committee room, or the seclusion of the private chamber, where business is prepared, and plans of public policy are elaborated and matured. Of this class of labors Mr. Ward sustained a large share. He entered into the duties of his station with a patriotic zeal, that shrank from no sacrifice of personal case, however great it might be. He was exceedingly regular in his attendance upon the House, and uniformly accepted, without hesitation, every work which was assigned to him to perform.

After the reassembling of the Congress in September, in addition to the service he almost daily rendered in the chair of the committee of the whole, he was appointed a member of the secret committee, to contract for arms and munitions of war, and of this committee he was subsequently chosen chairman. He was also a member of the standing committee on claims and accounts; a post which required his attention to an infinite number of details, and which compelled him to become conversant with all the operations of the army, and with the services performed by each of the respective colonies.

In addition to these two appointments, each of them of the most arduous and confining nature, he served upon a large number of special committees, some of which were charged with the most delicate and responsible duties. His colleague, Mr. Hopkins, was at this time disabled from writing, on account of physical infirmity; and the official correspondence of the delegation with the government and the citizens of the colony, was thus thrown wholly upon Mr. Ward. To the close confinement thus imposed upon him by the duties of his station, he makes frequent allusions in the familiar letters addressed to his family. In one of these, written in the month of October, he says, "I am almost worn out with attention to business. I am upon a standing committee of claims, which meets every morning before Congress, and upon the secret committee, which meets almost every afternoon; and these, with a close attendance upon Congress, and writing many letters, make my duty very hard, and I cannot get time to ride or take other exercise. But I hope the business will not be so pressing very long."

Our own times are so remote from the period of the American revolution, that we often are able to gain only an imperfect idea of the questions which perplexed the patriots of that day, or of the personal feelings with which they regarded the scenes that were passing before them. There were among them men of every hue of character, and every degree of decision; men who were prompted by impetuous temperaments, by selfish hopes, and by a high sense of duty; men who were timid champions of the cause, and were always hoping for a reconciliation, and those who staked their all upon the issue, who early saw that reconciliation was impossible, and were only waiting for the separation which they believed to be inevitable. In which of these classes of the patriots, who composed the Congress of the Confederation, Governor Ward deserves to be ranked, has already been indicated; it may, however, be more fully seen by the following extracts from familiar letters written to his brother in Rhode Island, during the autumn of 1775. On the 30th of September, he writes,

"No news from England since my last. The gentlemen of Georgia deserve the character I gave you of them; they are some of the highest sons of liberty I have seen, and are very sensible and clever. Mr. Wythe and Mr. Lee, of Virginia, have been under inoculation since my last, so that I can say no more of these than I did then. Saving that unhappy jealousy of New England, which some weak minds are possessed with, great unanimity prevails in Congress; our measures are spirited, and I believe we are now ready to go every length to secure our liberties. John Adams's letter [1] has silenced those, who opposed every decisive measure; but the moderate friends, or, as I consider them, the enemies of our cause, have caused copies of it to be sent throughout the province, in hopes, by raising the cry of independence, to throw the friends of liberty out of the new Assembly, the choice of which commences next Monday; but I believe they will fail, and that the House will be more decided than ever. One comfort we have, that divine wisdom and goodness often bring good out of ill. That the issue of this same contest will be the establishment of our liberties, I as firmly believe as I do my existence; for I never can think that God brought us into this wilderness to perish, or, what is worse, to become slaves, but to make us a great and free people."

On the 2d of November, he writes again in a strain equally characteristic.

"The evening before last, two ships arrived from England. The advices which they bring (amongst which is a proclamation for suppressing rebellion and sedition) are of immense service to us. Our councils have been hitherto too fluctuating; one day, measures for carrying on the war were adopted; the next, nothing must be done that would widen the unhappy breach between Great Britain and the colonies. As these different ideas have prevailed, our conduct has been directed accordingly. Had we, at the opening of the Congress in May, immediately taken proper measures for carrying on the war with vigor, we might have been in possession of all Canada, undoubtedly, and probably of Boston. Thank God, the happy day which I have long wished for is at length arrived; the southern colonies no longer entertain jealousies of the northern; they no longer look back to Great Britain; they are convinced that they have been pursuing a phantom, and that their only safety is a vigorous, determined defence. One of the gentlemen, who has been most sanguine for pacific measures, and very jealous of the New England colonies, addressing me in the style of *Brother Rebel*, told me he was now ready to join us heartily. 'We have got,' says he, 'a sufficient answer to our petition; I want nothing more, but am ready to declare ourselves independent, send ambassadors,' &c., and much more which prudence forbids me to commit to paper. Our resolutions will henceforth be spirited, clear, and decisive. May the Supreme Governor of the universe direct and prosper them!

"The pleasure which this unanimity gives me is inexpressible. I consider it a sure presage of victory. My anxiety is now at an end. I am no longer worried with contradictory resolutions, but feel a calm, cheerful satisfaction in having one great and just object in view, and the means of obtaining it certainly, by the divine blessing in our own hands."

Congress was at this time exceedingly perplexed and embarrassed on account of the condition of the army, the head-quarters of which were at Watertown. in Massachusetts. The troops had been enlisted, and brought into the service, under the authority of the colonies to which they respectively belonged; and the conditions of their enlistment, and the periods for which they were engaged to serve, were exceedingly various. Even after the appointment of the Commander-in-chief, and the other general officers, and the commencement of the Continental system, the men were still unwilling to serve far from home, or under any other than their own officers. The letters which General Washington addressed to the Congress, at this period, contain frequent allusions to the difficulties he constantly encountered in the arrangement of the army. In addition to the information thus communicated. Governor Ward held a correspondence with General Greene, from whom he obtained the most accurate views respecting its actual condition, and the difficulties inherent in its organization. His own letters are full of expressions of the solicitude he felt upon this subject, and they often refer to efforts which he made to induce Congress to take some decisive measures for averting the evils, which threatened the service of the country. [2]

The counsels of that body, however, were far from being unanimous respecting the extent to which the Continental system should be carried. Not a few of its members were exceedingly jealous of anything like an abridgment of the authority of the colonial governments, while others were for merging the whole of that authority, so far as the common cause was concerned, in the new central power which the exigencies of the times had called into being. These differences of opinion, and the feelings of jealousy and suspicion which were connected with them, enhanced the difficulty which attended the remodelling of the army, and filled the minds of those who were acquainted with its condition with the gravest apprehensions. Governor Ward was heartily in favor of the Continental system, and earnestly advocated the offering of a bounty by Congress in order to facilitate the enlistments: but he still thought that the attachment of the troops to their respective colonies was a matter too important to be broken up, or even disregarded, in framing the conditions of enlistment. He accordingly was exceedingly desirous that Congress, in building up its authority, and in regulating the military service of the country, should avoid every thing which might have a tendency to weaken the attachment, which the soldiers felt for the colonies to which they belonged.

His views upon this subject may be best learned from passages contained in the letters, which he addressed to his friends during the autumn of 1775, especially to his brother, the Secretary of State in Rhode Island. To this gentleman he writes, on the 21st of November.

"By letters from camp, I find there is infinite difficulty in reenlisting the army. The idea of making it wholly Continental has induced so many alterations, disgusting to both officers and men, that very little success has attended our recruiting orders. I have often told the Congress, that, under the idea of newmodelling, I was afraid we should destroy our army. Southern gentlemen wish to remove that attachment, which the officers and men have to their respective colonies, and make them look up to the continent at large for their support or promotion. I never thought that attachment injurious to the common cause, but the strongest inducement to people to risk everything in defence of the whole, upon the preservation of which must depend the safety of each colony. I wish, therefore, not to eradicate, but to regulate it in such a manner, as may most conduce to the protection of the whole.

"I am not a little alarmed at the present situation of the army. I wish your utmost influence may be used to put things upon a proper footing, and must beg leave through you to recommend the matter to the immediate attention of the Governor. There is no time to be lost."

The letters written at this period to Governor Ward, by General Greene, from the camp near Boston, breathe a similar spirit, and contain many facts, which were undoubtedly the basis of the views above given. The correspondence which Washington held not only with the Congress, but with the Governors and public men of several of the colonies, indicates how deep was his anxiety on account of the condition of the army, and how gloomy a period the autumn of 1775 must have been to all the far-sighted patriots of the revolution. It is from such sources as these that we derive the means of estimating aright the nature of the attachment which the people, especially in New England, felt for the respective colonies to which they belonged, and the difficulty with which this attachment was identified with their interest in the common cause of resistance to the ministry. Though great confidence was generally reposed in the wisdom of Congress, and high expectations were entertained concerning the results of its deliberations, yet the idea of a Continental sovereignty, independent of the authority of the colonies, was of slow growth in the popular mind, and the indistinctness with which it was conceived was a fertile source of embarrassment and confusion in the early stages of the revolution.

But events were steadily, though slowly, advancing towards the consummation which a few had anticipated from the beginning. The successive arrivals from England only confirmed the opinion, that the ministry were determined to persevere in enforcing the measures which they had adopted, and were preparing additional forces to decide the contest by the sword, in the approaching spring. In the meantime, some of the more active and fearless spirits in the colonies had conceived the idea of separation; and it was already beginning to spread among the people, though there might still be found those, who fondly clung to the hope of reconciliation. The wife of John Adams, writing from the heart of Massachusetts, was urging separation upon the mind of her husband with all the ardor of woman's eloquence. General Greene, in his letters to Governor Ward, many months before, had begun to recommend a declaration of independence, and had often declared that the people were beginning to wish for it. The Congress, however, was still inactive and uncertain in its opinions. The subject had not yet been discussed, nor had the word *Independence* been uttered in any of its debates. Its members, as they are described in the letters of John Adams, sat brooding " in deep anxiety and thoughtful melancholy," with only rare and remote allusions to the mighty question, and waiting for the occurrence of some critical event to decide their course of action.

Governor Ward, if we may judge from the tone of his letters, was more patient of this delay than were some others of the delegates from New England. He felt confident that independence would be the ultimate destiny of the colonies; and, when the troubles on account of the Stamp Act first appeared, he had often predicted this result in the friendly intercourse of private life. His most earnest desire was to see the different portions of the country united in the maintenance of their liberties, and to have the army thoroughly organized. With this preparation, he was willing patiently to wait the slow progress of events, and to leave the issue of all with the justice of Heaven.

The colony of Rhode Island was now suffering the worst evils consequent upon its exposed situation. The ships of the enemy, under the command of Captain Wallace, were lying along all its shore, and parties of marauders were constantly making depredations upon the property, and threatening the lives, of the inhabitants. Bristol had been attacked, and, after being laid under heavy contribution, was nearly destroyed. The Islands of Conanicut and Prudence had been ravaged with more than usual brutality; and the town of Newport, in which the British commander still had influential friends and supporters, was compelled to furnish periodical supplies to the fleet, which had exclusive control of the harbor and the adjacent bay. The commerce of the colony was entirely prostrate; some of the wealthiest inhabitants, refusing to engage in the revolution, had moved away, while the poor people, who remained, were reduced to the extremity of suffering by the severity of the winter, the scarcity of provisions, and the heavy restrictions, which were placed upon them. So large a portion of the men, who were fit for service, were enlisted in the Continental army, or were otherwise employed away from home, that those who remained were wholly insufficient for the protection of the long line of sea-coast, which bounded a large part of the colony.

In this general distress of the people, the Commander-in-chief, at the request of the Governor of Rhode Island, sent General Lee with a small detachment to Newport, to observe the condition of the town, and recommend such measures for its relief as he might deem practicable. The General Assembly passed an act making it a crime for any person to convey intelligence to the British ministry or their agents, to supply their armies or fleets with arms or military stores, or to serve as a pilot to an English vessel of war; and providing that whoever should be found guilty of the offence should be punished with death, and the confiscation of estate. [3] Several persons, who had rendered themselves obnoxious to this penalty, and who refused to make any promises for the future, were taken into custody, and their estates declared to be confiscated. The Assembly also adopted an address to Congress, in which they set forth, in the most urgent terms, the condition of the colony, the exertions which they had made, and were still making, for its defence, and their inability longer to sustain these exertions, or to keep the colony from falling into the hands of the enemy, unless they should receive timely aid from Congress. A copy of this address was forwarded to Mr. Ward at Philadelphia, and another was sent to General Washington, with a request that he would second the views which it contained, by such recommendation as his knowledge of the colony would enable him to give. [4]

The Commander-in-chief, when he communicated the paper to Congress, fully endorsed the statement it contained respecting the condition of the colony and the sufferings of its inhabitants, and expressed his conviction that it was highly necessary, that measures should be adopted to relieve their distress, and to furnish the aid they required. The delegates of Rhode Island did not immediately bring the address to the public attention of Congress, but preferred, according to the instructions which they received from the Governor of the colony, to consult some of the leading members upon the subject in private. A few weeks afterwards, Mr. Ward writes to Governor Cooke, that "this had been done; and from their generous concern for the colony, and a universal approbation of our vigorous exertions for the common defence, I have not the least doubt but the two battalions raised by the government will be taken into Continental pay."

The countenance which was received from General Washington, and the assurances of aid from Congress, together with the spirited acts of the Assembly, gave new energy to the people of the colony, and served to dissipate the gloom which had settled around their prospects. In Newport, the influential men, who still adhered to the ministry, and who maintained frequent intercourse with the British officers attached to the ships in the harbor, were thoroughly humbled by the visit of General Lee to the town, and by the bold stand which he took against them.

The peace of the town, however, was still almost entirely at the mercy of the British commander, whose numerous acts of insult and brutal violence in different parts of the colony called down upon his name and character the direst execrations of the people. In his moods of malice, which, it was said, were made more vindictive by frequent intoxication, he would often ravage the shores of Narragansett Bay, pillage the neighboring farms and hamlets, and sometimes take the lives of the inhabitants, in a manner that would be expected only of the outlaw chief of some horde of pirates. The distresses of his native colony, and especially of those portions of it with which, from infancy, he had been most familiar, enlisted the deepest sympathies of Governor Ward, and the numerous passages in his letters relating to the subject show how earnest were the efforts he made for their relief, both in Congress and in his communications to the colonial government.

[1] Two of the private letters of John Adams had been intercepted and published. The originals were sent to England, and are now in the State Paper Office in London. Mr. Sparks has published extracts from the originals, in *Washington's Writings*, Vol. II. p. 499. The one referred to in the text was addressed to James Warren, then President of the Provincial Congress of Massachusetts. See also *John Adams's Letters to his Wife*, Vol. I. p. 268.

[2] See Johnson's *Sketches of the Life and Character of General Greene*, Vol. I. p. 35 et seq.

[3] The town of Newport was excepted in this act, and, under certain restrictions, its people, in accordance with their own request, were allowed

to furnish supplies to the ships of Captain Wallace, which lay in their harbor. This was suffered as a measure of safety to the town, though its expediency was called in question in other parts of the colony, and by General Washington in his letter to Governor Cooke. Sparks's *Washington*, Vol. III. p. 227.

[4] This address, which bears the date of January 15th, 1776, together with the letter from General Washington to the President of Congress concerning it, is contained in the *American Archives*, Vol. V. p. 1148. It is a document of no small importance, as illustrating the exertions and the sufferings of the people of Rhode Island at this early stage of the revolution. From the account there presented, it appears that the colony, besides minute men and militia not yet called into service, had, at this time, not less than 3743 soldiers and sailors, exclusive of officers, in actual service, of whom 1700 were in the Continental army, and at least 200 more were on board armed vessels, beyond the limits of the colony. The whole population, in the year 1774, amounted to only 59,678 souls, and of these 5243 were Indians and Negroes. The number of families was 9437.

Chapter Eight

In September, 1775, a detachment of eleven hundred men had been sent, under the command of Colonel Benedict Arnold, on an expedition to Canada, for the purpose of weakening the British forces stationed there, and of conciliating the good will of the Canadians towards the cause of the colonies. When volunteers for this distant and perilous expedition were called for by General Washington, two hundred and fifty of the troops belonging to Rhode Island had presented themselves for the service. Among them was Samuel Ward, Junior, who, as we have already mentioned, had in the preceding spring received a captain's commission in the Continental army.

Upon the formation of the character of this young man, now in the twentieth year of his age. Governor Ward had bestowed the care which might naturally be expected of a fond and high-minded father. Having sent him to receive his classical education at the College of Rhode Island, he had seen him bear its highest honors at the period of his graduation, and, at the opening of the revolution, he had given him up, the hope and the pride of his family, to the service of his country. He had early instilled into his mind his own spirit of self-sacrificing patriotism, and had constantly enjoined upon him the practice of virtue and the fear of God.

After Captain Ward had joined the camp near Boston, and while the period of his enlistment was still undecided, his father wrote to him a letter, which contains a full expression of his views concerning the duty, which a citizen owes his country in times of calamity or distress. "With regard," says he, "to your engaging in the public service during the war, my sentiments are these; that so long as my country has any occasion for my service, and calls upon me properly, she has an undoubted right to it; and I shall ever esteem it the highest happiness to be able, in times of general distress, to do her any material good. Upon these principles, you will give me the highest satisfaction by devoting your life, while Heaven graciously continues it, to the public service. The poet justly said, '*Dulce et decorum est pro patria mori.*' I can as justly add, *pro patria vivere.*"

With these sentiments, rendered more forcible by parental example, to guide his conduct in the army, Captain Ward early attracted the notice of the Commander-in-chief, and, though at an immature age, he was permitted to join the troops from his native colony, who were commanded by his relative Colonel Christopher Greene, in the expedition to Quebec. Full of hope, and eager for the service in which they were to be engaged, the volunteers, under the command of Arnold, left the camp on the 15th of September, and arrived at the mouth of the Kennebec River on the 20th of the same month. Here they commenced their march through an untravelled wilderness, amidst the severities of an inclement season, without provisions, and but poorly clad; and, after enduring hardships such as were scarcely paralleled in all the struggle of the revolution, they reached the bank of the St. Lawrence, opposite Quebec, on the 15th of November. A few days from this date he writes to his sisters at Westerly.

"We were thirty days in a wilderness that none but savages ever attempted to pass. We marched one hundred miles upon short three days' provisions, waded over three rapid rivers, marched through snow and ice *barefoot*, passed over the St. Lawrence where it was guarded by the enemy's frigates, and are now about twenty-four miles from the city, to recruit our worn-out natures. General Montgomery intends to join us immediately, so that we have a winter's campaign before us; but I trust we shall have the glory of taking Quebec."

This expectation, which was also confidently entertained both in Congress and at the camp of the Commander-in-chief, was doomed to a melancholy disappointment. A few days after the arrival of Arnold, General Montgomery joined him on the plains before Quebec, with three hundred men from Montreal, and took command of the expedition. Though the force was still too small for the reduction of the city, yet the General, relying on the disposition of the Canadians to favor the cause of the Americans, commenced the attack on the morning of the 31st of December. The event proved but too clearly that this reliance was wholly misplaced. The heroic commander fell early in the battle, and his men were repulsed. The detachment led by Colonel Arnold was engaged at another point of the city. They had already forced one of the barriers, which had been thrown up for its defence, and were approaching a second, when Arnold was borne wounded from the ground. The troops, however, led on by Colonel Greene, were still maintaining the assault, when they were attacked in the rear, and their retreat cut off by a party of the enemy, and nearly four hundred of them were made prisoners. Among these were Captain Ward and a large portion of the company under his command.

On the 17th of January, 1776, the news reached Congress, by despatches from General Schuyler, of the disastrous fate of the expedition to Quebec, and of the fall of Montgomery. The intelligence was received with no common emotion. A brave officer, high in rank, had been snatched from the service of the country; and the hopes, which had been indulged that the people of Canada would join the colonies in their resistance to the ministry, were blighted at the very moment when they were the strongest and most ardent. But in the mind of no one in Congress, who on that day listened to the melancholy recital contained in the letters of General Schuyler, was a deeper anxiety excited, than in that of Governor Ward. As a warm-hearted patriot he mourned the loss of the gallant General, and, with a father's pride and a father's solicitude, he learned the heroic conduct and the unhappy fate of his son, the youthful captain, and his soldiers from Rhode Island. He was immediately appointed one of the committee to whom the communications of General Schuyler were referred; and on the 21st of January, so soon as the duties of the committee had been discharged, he addressed a letter to his son in Canada, which will illustrate his character both as a patriot and a father.

"My dear Son;

"I most devoutly thank God that you are alive, in good health, and have behaved well. You have now a new scene of action, to behave well as a prisoner. You have been taught from your infancy the love of God, of all mankind, and especially of your country; in a due discharge of these various duties of life consist true honor, religion, and virtue. I hope no situation or trial, however severe, will tempt you to violate those sound, immutable laws of God and nature. You will now have time for reflection; improve it well, and examine your own heart. Eradicate, as much as human frailty admits, the seeds of vice and folly. Correct your temper. Expand the benevolent feelings of your soul, and impress and establish the noble principles of private and public virtue so deeply in it, that your whole life may be directed by them. Next to these great and essential duties, improve your mind by the best authors you can borrow. Learn the French language, and be continually acquiring, as far as your situation admits, every useful accomplishment. Shun every species of debauchery and vice, as certain and inevitable ruin here and hereafter. There is one vice, which, though often to be met with in polite company, I cannot but consider as unworthy of a gentleman as well as a Christian. I mean swearing. Avoid it at all times.

"All ranks of people here have the highest sense of the great bravery and merit of Colonel Arnold, and all his officers and men. Though prisoners, they have acquired immortal honor. Proper attention will be paid to them. In the mean time, behave, my dear son, with great circumspection, prudence, and firmness. Enter into no engagements inconsistent with your duty to your country, and such as you may make keep inviolate with the strictest honor. Besides endeavoring to make yourself as easy and comfortable as possible in your present situation, you will pay the greatest attention, as far as your little power may admit, to the comfort and welfare of all your fellow-prisoners, and of those lately under your immediate command especially." [1]

During the winter of 1776, the attention of Congress was earnestly directed to preparation for the campaign, which it was expected the ensuing spring would open upon the country. The fall of Montgomery, and the failure of the expedition to Quebec, undoubtedly had a tendency to give a still more serious air to their deliberations. He was the first officer of the Continental army, high in rank, who had fallen in the service; and the fathers of the country mourned for him, as for one who had died an heroic martyr to the common cause. The committee, who were appointed to consider the subject, made a series of successive reports, which resulted in sending a deputation from Congress to visit Canada, and in reinforcing the army which was stationed there.

The military operations of the Continental army were also greatly extended; new posts were established, and arrangements set on foot for undertaking the defence of the entire continent, as the common territory of all the colonies was then termed. The attitude of Congress, however, had not changed. It was still that of deep anxiety and painful suspense, in which its members were waiting for some decisive event to determine the course they should adopt. Independence was only mentioned in the privacy of familiar intercourse, or in the correspondence of confidential friends. In the hall of Congress the word had not yet been uttered. But among those grave and thoughtful men, suspense was not a natural state of mind, and it could not long continue. Beneath the solemn exterior which they presented, a discerning eye might detect many a current of deep and earnest feeling, whose sure and silent flow was bearing the whole body insensibly onward to some mighty crisis.

These were the settled views, which now regulated the conduct and shaped the opinions of Governor Ward; and the familiar letters, which have guided us in framing this memoir, alone can show how deeply he was interested in the plans which Congress was now adopting, and in the approach of the events, which he felt confident were hastening on by the appointment of a destiny which no earthly power could withstand. He also, at this time, as was natural from the troubled condition of his native colony, experienced great anxiety on account of his domestic affairs. Eleven children had survived the death of their mother, which took place in 1770. Of these one had died during his attendance at the session of the first Congress. The three elder sons were now, in imitation of their father's example, in the service of the country, two of them holding places in the army, and one in the navy. The two elder daughters were recently married, and the remaining children, still of a tender age, were dwelling, without the protection of a parent, in the mansion at Westerly, in one of the most exposed situations along the coast of the colony. To that once cheerful and happy home of his family his thoughts would often revert, and his warm, parental affection would urge him to abandon the public service, that he might watch over the tender years of his children, and save from wasting and decay the beautiful estate which his industry had acquired.

But such were not the views of duty, which became a patriot statesman of the revolution. To him the present was of little importance; the future was all in all. Never, perhaps, in the history of mankind, has there been a period distinguished by so striking instances of the sacrifice of every private interest to the general good. The individual was but a unit in the mighty mass, whose freedom and happiness were of immeasurable importance. It was in accordance with this higher sentiment of duty to his country, that Governor Ward at this time decided against the dictates of parental affection, and resolved to remain in the Congress, and there abide the issues of the contest. In the month of February, of this long and anxious winter, he thus writes to the sister to whom he had especially committed the charge of his family.

"When I consider the alarms, the horrors and mischiefs of war, I cannot help thinking what those wretches deserve, who have involved this innocent country in all its miseries. At the same time, I adore the divine wisdom and goodness, which often overrules and directs those calamities to the producing of the greatest good. This I humbly hope will be our case. We may yet establish the peace and happiness of our native country upon the broad and never-failing basis of liberty and virtue.

"When I reflect upon this subject, and anticipate the glorious period, the dangers of disease, the inconveniences experienced in my private affairs, the almost unparalleled sufferings of Samuel [2] and all that my dear children and friends do or can suffer, appear to me trifling. I am sure your own love of liberty, and your fortitude of mmd, will not only support you, but will enable you to encourage and support all around you in the hour of danger. My dear little boys and girls, I know, need me much; but my duty forbids my return. I can only recommend them to God, to you, and my other sisters, and to their older sisters. Do all you possibly can to encourage them in the paths of virtue, industry, frugality, and neatness, and in improving their minds as far as their situation admits."

Such were the labors, the anxieties, and the hopes, which occupied the mmd of Governor Ward, when death, coming at an unexpected hour, suddenly put an end to them all. In the pressure of the many concerns, which had engaged his attention while in Congress, he had neglected to adopt the usual preventive against the smallpox, at that time one of the most dreaded of the diseases with which humanity could be afflicted. It frequently appeared with great malignity, especially in the large towns of the country; and Governor Ward had received repeated admonitions, while at Philadelphia, to resort to inoculation, the only preventive measure at that time known but though, as would appear from his letters, he dreaded the contagion with peculiar apprehension, he would never allow himself to be inoculated. [3]

In the Journal of Congress for the 13th of March is found the latest mention of his participation in the business of the House. On that day he presided in the committee of the whole, through a protracted discussion of several memorials and other papers relating to the trade of the colonies, and, on reporting to the House the progress of the debate, obtained leave to sit again. He also accepted an appointment as a member of a special committee, which was instructed to devise ways and means for defraying the anticipated expenses of the campaign that was soon to open. These duties, however, were not for him to perform.

On the two following days he was still in his place in Congress, with his characteristic punctuality and devotion to business. From this time his seat was vacant. The disease, which had already begun to be felt in his system, now appeared in its worst malignity, and on the 26th of March, 1776, put an end to his useful and honorable life, in the fifty-first year of his age. In the published "Letters" of John Adams, the event is thus noticed a few days after it happened.

"We have this week lost a very valuable friend of the colonies in Governor Ward, of Rhode Island, by the smallpox in the natural way. He never would hearken to his friends, who have been constantly advising him to be inoculated ever since the first Congress began. But he would not be persuaded. Numbers, who have been inoculated, have gone through this distemper without any danger, or even confinement. But nothing would do; he must take it in the natural way, and die. He was an amiable and a sensible man, a steadfast friend to his country, upon very pure principles. His funeral was attended with the same solemnities as Mr. Randolph's. Mr. Stillman, being the Anabaptist minister here, of which persuasion was the Governor, was desired by Congress to preach a sermon, which he did with great applause." [4]

He was interred in the burial-place of the First Baptist Church, amid the solemnities of religious worship, in the presence of the members of Congress, of the General Assembly of Pennsylvania, and a large concourse of the citizens of Philadelphia, among whom his amiable manners and exalted character had won for him many admiring friends. A monument was ordered to be erected to his memory at the place of his interment by a vote of Congress, and afterwards by an act of the General Assembly of Rhode Island.

The course of this memoir has furnished but few opportunities to refer to the religious opinions or the religious character of Governor Ward. He was, however, a sincere and humble Christian. He was connected, as were his ancestors before him, with a church of the Sabbatarian persuasion; a name given to what was then a large and highly respectable denomination of Christians in Rhode Island, who practised the rite of baptism by immersion, and adhered with singular tenacity to the ancient Jewish Sabbath as the appointed day of public worship. [5] He was at all times a careful observer of the simple forms of the church with which he was connected, and was withal a truly devout and conscientious, as well as a high-minded and honorable man.

His patriotism, which was deeply tinged with his religious feelings, was of the most constant and self-sacrificing nature. To be useful to the cause of American liberty, then struggling with mighty foes, to see his country successful in the great contest she had undertaken, and to win for himself the approbation of Heaven, "as a faithful servant and soldier of Jesus Christ," these, we may well judge, were the controlling aspirations of his mind, when death summoned him to the scenes of immortality, and to a nearer communion with the spiritual realities, which he had so long contemplated from afar.

His death took place on the eve of great events, which no man had more clearly foreseen, and which few men had done more to hasten forward. His sun went down ere the star of his country had risen, and while gloom and night yet hung round the whole horizon. Had his life been prolonged but for a little season, he would have beheld his native colony taking the lead of all the others in asserting the doctrines which he cherished, and becoming the first to throw off the allegiance that bound her to the British throne. [6] He would also have affixed his signature to the Declaration of American Independence, and thus linked with his name an enduring title to the gratitude of posterity, and won perhaps a prouder place in the annals of his country.

But this high guaranty of fame he was not permitted to attain; and we close this narrative of his life and services with the following estimate of his character, from the pen of one who knew him well, and who, while in Congress, relied with unwavering confidence on his fidelity, his wisdom, and his patriotism. The late John Adams, near the close of his venerable old age, in a letter dated January 29th, 1821, and addressed to one [7] of the descendants of Governor Ward, thus speaks of his character; "He was a gentleman in his manners, benevolent and amiable in his disposition, and as decided, ardent, and uniform in his patriotism, as any member of that Congress. When he was seized with the smallpox, he said that if his vote and voice were necessary to support the cause of his country, he should live, if not, he should die. He died, and the cause of his country was supported, but it lost one of its most sincere and punctual advocates."

The life of Governor Ward was abruptly closed at a gloomy period in the history of his country. But his generous patriotism and his manly spirit did not die. He had instilled them with parental care into the mind of the son who bore his name, and to whose early service in the army of the revolution we have already alluded. The father descended to the tomb in the meridian of his days, but the leading features of his character were inherited by the son, who in his own career worthily exemplified the precepts and counsels which had guided his youth.

Samuel Ward, Junior, was born at Westerly, on the 17th of November, 1756. He was graduated at Brown University, with distinguished honors, in the class of 1771. At the early age of eighteen, he received a Captain's commission from the government of his native colony, and in May, 1775, marched with his company to join the army of observation, which Rhode Island was at that time raising for her own and the common defence. In the autumn of the same year he volunteered, with a large body of the troops of Rhode Island, to accompany Colonel Arnold on the expedition to Quebec, an expedition attended with sufferings and privations such as were scarcely surpassed, if indeed they were equalled, during the war. They were bravely encountered and heroically endured; but the expedition terminated in disaster and defeat. With a large number of his gallant associates, Captain Ward was overpowered by superior force, taken prisoner, and carried to Quebec, where he was still detained at the period of his father's death.

In the course of the year 1776, he was exchanged, and, on his return to Rhode Island, married the daughter of William Greene, of Warwick, who was afterwards Governor of that state. Soon after his exchange. Captain Ward was commissioned as Major in the regiment of Colonel Christopher Greene, who had been his brave associate in the toils and disasters of the expedition to (Quebec. Under this gallant commander he bore a distinguished part in the celebrated battle at Red Bank, in which Fort Mercer was successfully defended from the assault of the Hessians under Count Donop. Of this action, at the order of his Colonel, he drew up the official account, which was forwarded to the Commander-in-chief, and which is now contained in the published correspondence of General Washington. [8] He was also in the camp of Washington during the dreadful winter in which the army was quartered at Valley Forge.

In 1778, the regiment of Colonel Greene was detached for special service in the colony to which it belonged, and was placed under the command of General Sullivan, whose headquarters were then at Providence. The General was preparing an expedition, which he had been ordered to undertake against the island of Rhode Island, for the purpose of dislodging the British forces, and driving them from the shores of Narragansett Bay. In this expedition Mr. Ward, though holding only a Major's commission, was intrusted with the command of a regiment. The enterprise proved unsuccessful, and the army of General Sullivan was obliged to retreat from the island; but the youthful officer, though charged with a responsibility above his commission, behaved with prudence and gallantry, and contributed his share to the order and success with which the retreat, so mortifying to the commander, and so calamitous to the colony, was conducted.

In April of the following year, he received the commission of Lieutenant-Colonel in the first regiment of the division from Rhode Island; and in this command he passed two years in Washington's army, while stationed in New Jersey, and upon Hudson's River. In many of the important operations of this period he bore the part becoming to his rank; he endured patiently the toils and privations which the service of his country imposed upon the army, and won for himself a share of the glory which belongs to all those, who, amidst disappointment, disaster, and the keenest suffering, were still faithful to the cause of the revolution.

Near the close of the war. Colonel Ward retired from the army, and engaged in mercantile pursuits in the city of New York. While thus employed, he made several voyages to Europe and the East Indies, and was among the first to display the flag of his country in the China Seas. He also resided in Paris during some of the early stages of the French revolution, and was present at the scene when Louis the Sixteenth was beheaded. On his return to the United States, he retired from the mercantile house with which he had been long connected, and settled with his family on an estate near East Greenwich, in Rhode Island. Here, amid the quiet pursuits of agriculture, he revived the studies of his early years, and to the end of his life maintained a scholar's familiarity with Caesar, Ovid, and Horace, the classic writers, who had been the favorites of his academic days. On the death of his wife, in the year 1817, he removed to Jamaica, in the vicinity of New York. Here and in the metropolis itself, where some of his children were now settled in business, he lived for many years in the enjoyment of congenial society, and blessed with the filial love of a numerous family, and with the confidence and respect of a wide circle of friends.

Colonel Ward, though well qualified for public life by his talents and education, as well as by his varied experience of human affairs, and his familiar acquaintance with most of the leading men of the country, yet was too strongly attached to the quiet scenes of his own home, and was withal too little ambitious of political distinction, ever to engage with relish in the exciting labors of the politician. He was twice, however, chosen to represent his fellow citizens in what were then deemed important public bodies. One of them was the commercial convention which assembled at Annapolis, in 1786; the other was the Convention which met at Hartford in 1812.

With these solitary exceptions, his days were passed in the humble occupations of a private gentleman. Yet he was not indifferent to the fortunes of his country. He had been taught to love her from his infancy, and had spent the first years of his early manhood in the achievement of her independence. But now that this had been secured, he yielded to the love of quiet inherent in his nature, and felt at liberty to keep himself aloof from her public concerns. He died at New York, in 1832, at the age of seventy-five years.

The recollection of the person and the character of Colonel Ward is still vivid in the minds of many, who knew him as he appeared in society, in the later years of his life. One of these, who can well judge of the qualities he specifies, has pronounced him to have been "a ripe classical scholar, a gentleman of most winning urbanity of manners, and a man of sterling intellect and unblemished honor." [9]

[1] The letter, from which this is an extract, was published in the *American Annual Register,* Vol. VII. p. 407.
[2] His son, Captain Ward, now a prisoner at Quebec.
[3] He is said to have had an invincible repugnance to this mode of taking the disease. Indeed, a strong prejudice had always existed in the colonies against inoculation, since its first introduction in 1721. Vaccination was first adopted in England, by Dr. Jenner, in 1798, and was introduced into America, about the year 1800, through the agency of Dr. Benjamin Waterhouse, a native of Newport, and at that time a lecturer at Harvard College, and also at Brown University.
[4] John Adams's *Letters to his Wife*, Vol. I. p. 92.
[5] Among his papers is a confession of his faith in the fundamental doctrines of Christianity, which was submitted to the church on his admission as a member.
[6] The act of allegiance was repealed by the General Assembly in May, 1776.
[7] Richard R. Ward, Esq., of New York.
[8] Sparks's *Washington,* Vol. V. p. 112.
[9] Notices of the early Graduates at Brown University, by William G. Goddard.

www.ingramcontent.com/pod-product-compliance
Lightning Source LLC
Chambersburg PA
CBHW021941040426
42448CB00008B/1175